James Swofford
University of South Alabama

STUDY GUIDE

to accompany

Modern Principles:
MICROECONOMICS

second edition

Tyler Cowen ▲ Alex Tabarrok

WORTH PUBLISHERS

Study Guide
by James Swofford
to accompany
Cowen/Tabarrok: *Modern Principles: Microeconomics, Second Edition*

ISBN 13: 978-1-4292-8954-2
ISBN 10: 1-4292-8954-6

First Printing 2011

Printed in the United States of America

Worth Publishers
41 Madison Avenue
New York, NY 10010
www.worthpublishers.com
www.wortheconomics.com

Contents

Key to Corresponding Chapter Numbers

	Microeconomics	Economics	Macroeconomics
The Big Ideas	Chapter 1	Chapter 1	Chapter 1
The Power of Trade and Comparative Advantage	Chapter 2	Chapter 2	Chapter 2
Supply and Demand	Chapter 3	Chapter 3	Chapter 3
Equilibrium: How Supply and Demand Determine Prices	Chapter 4	Chapter 4	Chapter 4
Elasticity and its Applications	Chapter 5	Chapter 5	
Taxes and Subsidies	Chapter 6	Chapter 6	
The Price System: Signals, Speculation and Prediction	Chapter 7	Chapter 7	
Price Ceilings and Price Floors	Chapter 8	Chapter 8	Chapter 5
International Trade	Chapter 9	Chapter 9	Chapter 19
Externalities: When Prices Send the Wrong Signals	Chapter 10	Chapter 10	
Costs and Profit Maximization Under Competition	Chapter 11	Chapter 11	
Competition and the Invisible Hand	Chapter 12	Chapter 12	
Monopoly	Chapter 13	Chapter 13	
Price Discrimination	Chapter 14	Chapter 14	
Cartels, Oligopolies, and Monopolistic Competition	Chapter 15	Chapter 15	
Competing for Monopoly: The Economics of Network Goods	Chapter 16	Chapter 16	
Labor Markets	Chapter 17	Chapter 17	
Public Goods and the Tragedy of the Commons	Chapter 18	Chapter 18	
Political Economy and Public Choice	Chapter 19	Chapter 19	Chapter 21
Economics, Ethics and Public Policy	Chapter 20	Chapter 20	
Managing Incentives	Chapter 21	Chapter 21	
Stock Markets and Personal Finance	Chapter 22	Chapter 22	Chapter 10

	Microeconomics	Economics	Macroeconomics
Consumer Choice	Chapter 23	Chapter 23	
GDP and the Measurement of Progress		Chapter 24	Chapter 6
The Wealth of Nations and Economic Growth		Chapter 25	Chapter 7
Growth, Capital Accumulation and the Economics of Ideas: Catching Up vs. The Cutting Edge		Chapter 26	Chapter 8
Saving, Investment, and the Financial System		Chapter 27	Chapter 9
Unemployment and Labor Force Participation		Chapter 28	Chapter 11
Inflation and the Quantity Theory of Money		Chapter 29	Chapter 12
Business Fluctuations: Aggregate Demand and Supply		Chapter 30	Chapter 13
Transmission and Amplification Mechanisms		Chapter 31	Chapter 14
The Federal Reserve System and Open Market Operations		Chapter 32	Chapter 15
Monetary Policy		Chapter 33	Chapter 16
The Federal Budget: Taxes and Spending		Chapter 34	Chapter 17
Fiscal Policy		Chapter 35	Chapter 18
International Finance		Chapter 36	Chapter 20

Preface

This ***Study Guide*** is designed for use with the second edition of ***Modern Principles: Microeconomics*** by Tyler Cowen and Alex Tabarrok. Economics is not just an interesting subject for study, but is an integral part of life used in everything from shopping at the local grocery store to buying a house to understanding national and local legislation. To help you reach your goal of understanding economics, this study guide includes a number of exercises that involve self-testing and repetition. Together, these activities will enhance your learning of text material and will help you to evaluate your understanding of important concepts.

Have you ever taken a test thinking you were well prepared only to discover that you really didn't understand a particular concept? Ideally, working through each study guide chapter will enable you to actively learn the text chapter's contents while also discovering and focusing on material you thought you had mastered but had not.

Learning Objectives, Summary and Key Terms

Each chapter begins by setting out learning objectives from the textbook chapter. These learning objectives are immediately followed by a chapter summary containing the essential points of the chapter, including useful tables and graphs from the text. To make the material easier for you to digest, the summary is deliberately brief and straightforward. Reading the summary does not replace reading the text. However, reading the summary can help solidify your understanding of the text material.

For your convenience, the key terms in the text chapter are listed separately and defined again.

Traps, Hints, and Reminders

These short sections first identify concepts that from experience we have found can be difficult for undergraduate students that are new to economics as a subject of study. Helpful hints for understanding that material are then provided. The section also includes information about concepts that we think are among the most important.

Homework Quiz and Self-Practice Questions

When you feel comfortable that you understand the chapter contents, try to complete the 25 multiple-choice homework questions. Your instructor has the correct answers to these questions.

Each study guide chapter also contains a self-test review, which includes about 25 multiple-choice questions. Answers are provided at the end of the chapter. This self-test review is yet another opportunity for active learning.

Acknowledgements

A number of people and institutions have greatly facilitated the process of me writing both the first and second editions of this study guide. I want to thank the University of South Alabama, Mobile, Alabama for granting me a sabbatical leave during the fall term of 2009. Thanks also go to the department of economics of Lund University in Lund, Sweden, that invited me to be a visiting scholar during my sabbatical. In addition to getting scholarly work done while in Sweden, my visit to Lund gave me time away from the usual distractions of life to get a very good jump on writing the first edition of this study guide.

I would also like to thank my wife, Cindy, who put the eyes of a non-economist on each chapter and found many places to help make this study guide more readable. I would like to thank my colleague Mitch Mitchell who shared ideas and encouraged me.

Finally, I would also like to thank the entire Worth staff who facilitated my participation in this project. I would like to thank Tom Kling and Paul Shensa for all their encouragement and Tom Acox who worked the closest with me on writing and formatting the chapters.

Jim Swofford, 2011
Spanish Fort, Alabama

1

The Big Ideas

Learning Objectives

The objective of this chapter is for you to learn about a number of big ideas of economics that are the overarching ideas that occur and reoccur throughout the book. The big ideas include:

> Incentives Matter
> Good Institutions Align Self-Interest with the Social Interest
> Trade-offs Are Everywhere
> Thinking on the Margin
> The Power of Trade
> The Importance of Wealth and Economic Growth
> Institutions Matter
> Economic Booms and Busts Cannot Be Avoided But They Can Be Moderated
> Prices Rise When the Government Prints Too Much Money
> Central Banking Is a Hard Job
> The Biggest Idea of All: Economics Is Fun

Summary

Incentives are rewards and penalties that motivate behavior, and they matter. For example, if you pay unemployed people longer, then the unemployment rate will remain higher than it otherwise would be. Good institutions align self-interest with the social interest. The market often does this in a manner for which Adam Smith coined the term, "the invisible hand." The farmer works hard on his farm, the trucker takes food from farm to market, the grocer takes risks and opens a store. All these people do these things in their own self-interest (to make money for themselves), not to make sure that you do not starve. Yet you and society benefit from their self-interest. Put more crudely, greed is often good.

Trade-offs are everywhere. You cannot have your cake and eat it, too. You must make a choice. The value of a lost opportunity is the **opportunity cost** of a choice: If you eat your cake now, you must give up having it later; if you save the cake for later, you have to give up eating it now. In order to understand trade-offs, you need to think on the margin. Thinking on the margin is thinking in terms of small changes. Examples include marginal cost, which is the change in cost when a firm produces one more of its product, and marginal revenue, which is the change in revenue when the firm sells one less of its product.

The power of trade is that trade and specialization allow people to produce more than they could otherwise. Trade takes place when both parties expect to and usually do gain. It also allows people to consume more than they can produce. It can even take place between the highly productive and the not-very-productive because of the concept of comparative advantage, the ability to produce at a lower opportunity cost than your trading partner. Trade leads to economic growth and wealth, which in turn leads to better lives for people—economic growth and wealth are associated with a longer life expectancy and lower infant mortality.

Institutions matter and affect economic growth and wealth. Countries that are similar but have differing institutions can vary widely in wealth and economic growth. The institutions that support good incentives are property rights, political stability, honest government, a dependable legal system, and competitive and open markets.

Economic booms and busts cannot be avoided but they can be moderated. Some economic shocks, for example, earthquakes and bad weather, cannot be avoided. But other important shocks that have contributed to "busts," for example, the Great Depression of the 1930s, have been due to bad economic policy and could have been avoided. In the 1930s, however, economic fiscal and monetary policies were less well understood than they are today. The current better understanding of both types of policy can and should help moderate booms and busts.

Central banking is a hard job. The U.S. central bank is called the Federal Reserve, or, simply, the Fed. Central banks must deal with an uncertain future, calls for them to accomplish more than they actually can, make policy today that affects the economy with a time lag, and face conflicting goals. If the central bank puts too little money in circulation, the economy can go into recession. If the central bank errs on the other side and prints too much money, prices rise.

The biggest idea of all is that *economics is fun*. We are surrounded by economics. It can tell us why some countries are rich and some are poor. It can tell us about how to reduce crime, or how to manage a business, or how to set up good incentives for government.

Key Terms

incentives rewards and penalties that motivate behavior

opportunity cost cost of a choice is the value of the opportunities lost

inflation a general increase in prices

Traps, Hints, and Reminders

Opportunity cost is a trap for students because it includes both explicit, or out-of-pocket costs, and implicit costs, ones that are not actually paid out of pocket.

Remember, when it says "See the Invisible Hand" in the book's margins, the authors are referring to the big idea that good institutions align self-interest with the social interest.

Marginal analysis involves changing by small units. Many later chapters also discuss marginal analysis. The term "marginal" means incremental or small change.

Comparative advantage is the ability to produce at a lower opportunity cost than another producer can. This allows a less productive producer to still be able to trade with a highly productive one.

Trade takes place when both sides expect to gain, which is what usually happens. Despite what people sometimes seem to think, no one *has* to lose in a trade.

Economist Milton Friedman has pointed out that "inflation is always and everywhere a monetary phenomenon"; in other words, inflation happens when the central bank prints too much money.

Central banks cannot do everything. There are really only a limited number of things they can do, but they *can*, first and foremost, provide a stable price level for the economy.

Homework Quiz

激励

1. Incentives are

   处罚   激发行为

   a. rewards and penalties that motivate behavior.

   b. what one gives to charity.

   c. behaviors that motivate rewards or penalties.

   d. the value of opportunities lost.

与…保持一致   意味着

2. The idea that good institutions can align self-interest and social interest implies that

   a. the government should control the market.

   b. sometimes self-interest or greed is good.

   c. consumers need government help to choose what to buy.

   d. firms need government help to choose what to produce.

3. The phrase that Adam Smith used to describe a situation in which self-interest promotes social interest is

   a. "greed is good."

   b. "the cost of opportunity."

   c. "the invisible hand."

   d. "thinking on the margin."

4. Opportunity cost is

   a. the change in costs when output changes.

   b. the money you spend on a product.

   c. the value of the time you give up consuming a product.

   d. the value of the opportunities lost.

5. If for this term your tuition is $5,000, your books are $1,000, you pay $4,000 for room and board, and you work part time, making $5,000 rather than $10,000 for the term, your opportunity costs of attending college this term are

   a. $5,000.

   b. $10,000.

   c. $11,000.

   d. $15,000.

6. A trade-off associated with more testing of a drug before it can be sold is that

   a. the drug is safer for consumers.

   b. some people are harmed before the drug can be sold.

   c. some people are harmed after the drug can be sold.

   d. the drug is less safe for consumers.

7. If you go to an all-you-can-eat pizza buffet, pay $5 for the buffet, and then eat 5 slices of pizza, the marginal cost of the second slice of pizza is

a. $0.

b. $1.

$5 /5 = $1

c. $2.

d. $5.

8. Two people trade when they expect that

a. the seller will be better off, while the buyer will be worse off.

b. the buyer will be better off, while the seller will be worse off.

c. each will be worse off.

d. each will be better off.

9. Trade can benefit

a. only the productive.

b. only the rich.

c. even those who are not particularly productive.

d. only sellers.

10. According to the authors, wealth and economic growth are associated with

a. lower infant mortality rates.

b. higher church attendance.

c. an increased prison population.

d. All of the answers are correct.

11. Since 1950, South Korea has grown much more than North Korea has because

a. South Korea was the richer country in 1950.

b. capitalist countries are conspiring against North Korea.

c. South Korea has institutions that provide incentives for innovation and investment.

d. North Korea is too mountainous for companies to build factories.

12. According to your text, the Great Depression was

a. prolonged by bad policy.

b. a natural occurrence in a capitalist society.

c. caused by a famine in India.

d. caused by the beginning of World War II.

13. The central bank of the United States is called

a. Bank of America.

b. the National Bank of the United States.

c. the Federal Reserve.

d. Washington Mutual.

14. When the central bank prints too much money
   a. people cannot get paper anymore.
   b. inflation occurs.
   c. prices fall too fast.
   d. All of the answers are correct.

15. Central banking is a hard job because
   a. printing money is a complicated business.
   b. the future of the economy is unpredictable.
   c. the central bank has little influence over inflation.
   d. there are not enough challenges to make central banking interesting.

Self-Practice Questions

1. One incentive a business can offer a customer to buy its product is
   a. a lower price.
   b. a better product.
   c. better service.
   d. All of these are incentives.

2. Good institutions
   a. eliminate trade-offs.
   b. align self-interest with the social interest.
   c. eliminate incentives.
   d. eliminate self-interest.

3. The phrase "invisible hand" refers to
   a. opportunity costs.
   b. when self-interest promotes social interest.
   c. what is sacrificed for a choice.
   d. the central bank.

4. Opportunity cost is
   a. the reward for a behavior.
   b. one reason central banking is hard.
   c. the value of an opportunity lost.
   d. the invisible hand.

5. If this term your tuition is $20,000, your books cost $1,000, you pay $10,000 for room and board, and you work part time, making $5,000 rather than $10,000 this term, your opportunity costs of attending college this term are

   a. $21,000.

   b. $26,000.

   c. $31,000.

   d. $36,000.

6. A example of a marginal choice would be

   a. whether to hire one more worker.

   b. the value of opportunity lost.

   c. the invisible hand.

   d. whether to enter a business.

7. Trade can increase production by means of

   a. getting the better of the other party.

   b. specialization.

   c. protection.

   d. All of the answers are correct.

8. Countries become wealthy due to:

   a. conquests.

   b. government.

   c. economic growth.

   d. environmental controls.

9. Inflation is

   a. economic growth.

   b. an increase in wealth.

   c. an increase in the price level.

   d. an increase in employment.

10. According to your text, the Great Depression

   a. could have been moderated by better economic policies.

   b. was a natural occurrence in a capitalist society.

   c. was caused by free trade.

   d. was caused by the U.S. Civil War.

11. Booms and busts cannot be completely avoided because of

   a. economic policy mistakes.

   b. shocks to economies, like destructive weather or earthquakes.

   c. international trade.

   d. incentives.

12. The central bank has a hard job because

    a. of time lags between policy changes and effects in the economy.

    b. it is difficult to foresee the future.

    c. it often has conflicting goals.

    d. All of the answers are correct.

13. When prices are rising in general, such a rise is known as

    a. a boom.

    b. inflation.

    c. rationing.

    d. appreciation.

14. Among the most powerful institutions for supporting good incentives are

    a. property rights.

    b. protection.

    c. monopoly.

    d. government intervention in markets.

15. The principles of economics hold

    a. only for businesses.

    b. only in capitalist countries.

    c. only in western countries.

    d. everywhere.

Answers to Self-Practice Questions

1. d, Topic: Incentives Matter

2. b, Topic: Good Institutions Align Self-Interest with the Social Interest

3. b, Topic: Good Institutions Align Self-Interest with the Social Interest

4. c, Topic: Trade-offs Are Everywhere

5. b, Topic: Trade-offs Are Everywhere

6. a, Topic: Thinking on the Margin

7. b, Topic: The Power of Trade

8. c, Topic: The Importance of Wealth and Economic Growth

9. c, Topic: Prices Rise When the Government Prints Too Much Money

10. a, Topic: Economic Booms and Busts Cannot Be Avoided But They Can Be Moderated

11. b, Topic: Economic Booms and Busts Cannot Be Avoided But They Can Be Moderated

12. d, Topic: Central Banking Is a Hard Job

13. b, Topic: Prices Rise When the Government Prints Too Much Money

14. a, Topic: The Importance of Wealth and Economic Growth

15. d, Topic: The Biggest Idea of All: Economics Is Fun

2

The Power of Trade and Comparative Advantage

Learning Objectives

The objective of this chapter is for you to learn about comparative advantage and the power of trade. Topics covered include:

> Trade and Preferences

> Specialization, Productivity, and the Division of Knowledge

> Comparative Advantage

> Trade and Globalization

The purpose of this chapter is for you to learn about the gains from trade.

Summary

Trade makes people with different preferences better off. Trade transfers a good to the buyer, who values the good more than the money it costs; and trade transfers money back to the seller, who values the money more than the good he or she gave up.

Trade allows people to specialize in production and take advantage of a division of knowledge. People will only specialize in the production of a single good when they are confident that they can trade that good for the many other goods they want. Without trade, specialization would be impossible.

Division of knowledge is also important in allowing people to specialize—each individual would need only to know more about his or her one specific area of knowledge. The farmer needs only to know about farming, the attorney needs to only know about the law, and the chef needs only to know about cooking. Without specialization, a person running a restaurant would have to know enough about farming to grow crops, know enough about the law to set up his or her business enterprise, and know enough about food preparation to be the chef.

Absolute advantage is the ability to produce a good using fewer inputs. Absolute advantage, however, is not required for trade. **Comparative advantage** is the ability to produce at the lowest opportunity cost. Every individual will have a comparative advantage in something, even if he or she does not have an absolute advantage in any one good. This applies to people individually and to the people of a country. Exploiting comparative advantage can be summed up as: sell what costs you a low amount to make and buy what would cost you a lot to make.

Absolute and comparative advantage can be illustrated by using a **production possibilities frontier (PPF)**. A production possibilities frontier shows all the combinations of goods that can be produced given productivity and the supply of inputs or resources. Figure 2.1 shows the PPF for the production of shirts and computers in Mexico and the United States.

Figure 2.1

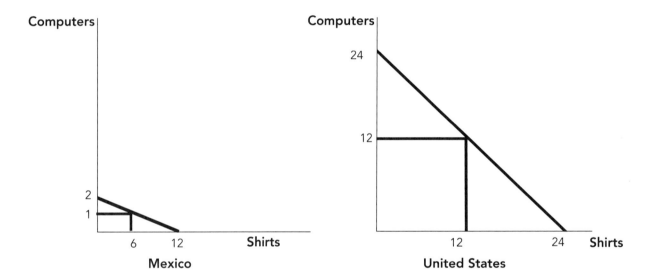

The graph on the left in Figure 2.1 shows that the Mexicans can produce either 2 computers and 0 shirts or 0 computers and 12 shirts. Thus, in Mexico, the opportunity cost of 1 computer is 6 shirts and the opportunity cost of 1 shirt is one-sixth of a computer. The graph on the right shows that Americans can produce 24 computers and 0 shirts or 0 computers and 24 shirts. Thus, in the United States the opportunity cost of 1 computer is 1 shirt or the opportunity cost of 1 shirt is 1 computer. These data are summarized in Table 2.1, in which the production columns summarize each country's situation if it produces only one of the two goods.

If there is no trade, both Mexico and the United States must consume what they each produce. Mexico could choose to produce and consume 1 computer and 6 shirts, while the United States could choose to produce and consume 12 computers and 12 shirts. That makes the total production and consumption of both countries 13 computers and 18 shirts. The no-trade position is summarized in Table 2.2.

Table 2.1 Opportunity Costs

Country	Production of Only Computers	Production of Only Shirts	Opportunity Cost of One Computer	Opportunity Cost of One Shirt
Mexico	2	12	6 shirts	1/6 computer
United States	24	24	1 shirt	1 computer

Table 2.2 Production 5 Consumption in Mexico and the United States (Specialization with No Trade)

	Production of Computers	Consumption of Computers	Production of Shirts	Consumption of Shirts
Mexico	1	1	6	6
United States	12	12	12	12
Total	13	13	18	18

Trade can improve the no-trade total result of 13 computers and 18 shirts. Mexico can shift its production to 0 computers and 12 shirts, while the United States can shift its production to 15 computers and 9 shirts. (Notice that both of these points are on the PPF of the respective countries in Table 2.1.) This makes the total production of Mexico and the United States 15 computers and 21 shirts, which is larger than the total production with no trade.

If the United States trades 2 computers to Mexico for 4 shirts, then Mexico consumes 2 computers and 8 shirts, while the United States consumes 13 computers and 14 shirts. Thus, with trade, Mexicans consume 1 more computer and 2 more shirts compared to with no trade, while Americans consume 1 more computer and 2 more shirts compared to with no trade. These results are summarized in Table 2.3.

Table 2.3 Production and Consumption in Mexico and the United States (Specialization and Trade)

	Production of Computers	Consumption of Computers	Production of Shirts	Consumption of Shirts
Mexico	0	2 (+1)	12	8 (+2)
United States	15	13 (+1)	9	13 (+1)
Total	15	15	21	21

As we have seen in the preceding table, both the United States and Mexico gained from trade. That is, they were able to consume at points outside their PPFs.

Key Terms

absolute advantage the ability to produce a good using fewer inputs than your trading partner.

comparative advantage the ability to produce a good at a lower opportunity cost than your trading partner

production possibilities frontier (PFF) what can be produced given productivity and the supply of inputs

Traps, Hints, and Reminders

Notice that both sides can gain from trade; that is, no one has to get the better of the other when trading. In fact, trade only takes place when both parties expect to gain, and both sides usually do gain.

Comparative advantage means that even if you are bad at everything you can still trade. There will be something you are the least worst at; that is, you will be able to produce that thing at the lowest opportunity cost.

Homework Quiz

1. If you can produce a good at the lowest opportunity costs, then you have
   a. an absolute advantage.
   b. a comparative advantage.
   c. an unfair advantage.
   d. All of the answers are correct.

2. You have an absolute advantage in producing goods that you can produce
   a. more of.
   b. at the lowest opportunity cost.
   c. using fewer resources.
   d. All of the answers are correct.

3. Everyone must necessarily have
   a. a comparative advantage.
   b. an absolute advantage.
   c. a tariff.
   d. All of the answers are correct.

Table 2.4

Country	Production of Only Cameras	Production of Only Computers	Opportunity Cost of Cameras	Opportunity Cost of One Computer
United States	3	5	$\frac{5}{3}$	$\frac{3}{5}$
Japan	2	2	1	1

4. According to the data in Table 2.4, the opportunity cost of a computer in the United States is

   a. 0.6 camera.

   b. 1 camera.

   c. 1.67 cameras.

   d. None of the answers is correct.

5. According to the data in Table 2.4, the opportunity cost of a camera in Japan is

   a. 0.6 computer.

   b. 1 computer.

   c. 1.67 computers.

   d. None of the answers is correct.

6. According to the data in Table 2.4, if both countries have the same resources, Japan has an absolute advantage in producing

   a. cameras.

   b. computers.

   c. both goods.

   d. neither good.

7. According to the data in Table 2.4, the United States has a comparative advantage in producing

   a. cameras.

   b. computers.

   c. both goods.

   d. neither good.

8. According to the data in Table 2.4, Japan has a comparative advantage in producing

   a. cameras.

   b. computers.

   c. both goods.

   d. neither good.

9. A production possibility frontier shows what the people of the area
   a. want to consume.
   b. can produce.
   c. want to produce.
   d. must produce.

Figure 2.2

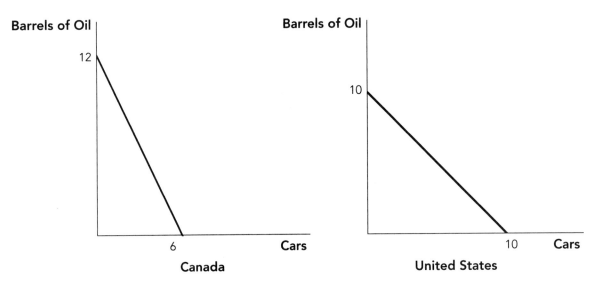

Canada   United States

10. In Figure 2.2, if both countries have the same resources, Canada has an absolute advantage in producing
    a. oil.
    b. cars.
    c. both oil and cars.
    d. neither oil nor cars.

11. In Figure 2.2, the opportunity cost of oil in Canada is
    a. 0.5 car.
    b. 1 car.
    c. 2 cars.
    d. 6 cars.

12. In Figure 2.2, the opportunity cost of cars in Canada is
    a. 0.5 barrel of oil.
    b. 1 barrel of oil.
    c. 2 barrels of oil.
    d. 10 barrels of oil.

13. In Figure 2.2, the opportunity cost of cars in the United States is
    a. 0.5 barrel of oil.   c. 2 barrels of oil.
    b. 1 barrel of oil.   d. 10 barrels of oil.

14. In Figure 2.2, Canada has a comparative advantage in producing

a. oil.   c. both oil and cars.

b. cars.   d. neither oil nor cars.

15. In Figure 2.2, the United States has a comparative advantage in producing

a. oil.

b. cars.

c. both oil and cars.

d. neither oil nor cars.

oil: $\frac{6}{12} = \frac{1}{2} < 1$

car = $\frac{12}{6} > 1$

Self-Practice Questions

1. You have a comparative advantage in producing goods that you can produce

a. more of.

b. at the lowest opportunity cost.

c. using fewer inputs.

d. All of the answers are correct.

2. If you can produce a good using fewer resources, then you have

a. an unfair advantage.

b. a comparative advantage.

c. an absolute advantage.

d. All of the answers are correct.

3. To trade, you must at least have

a. a wage advantage.

b. an absolute advantage.

c. a tariff.

d. a comparative advantage.

Table 2.5

Country	Production of Only Cheese	Production of Only Computers	Opportunity Cost of One Cheese	Opportunity Cost of One Computer
United States	2	4	2	$\frac{1}{2}$
France	3	1	$\frac{1}{3}$	3

4. According to the data in Table 2.5, the opportunity cost of cheese in the United States is

a. 0.33 computer.   c. 2 computers.

b. 0.5 computer.   d. 3 computers.

5. According to the data in Table 2.5, the opportunity cost of cheese in France is
   a. 0.33 computer.
   b. 0.5 computer.
   c. 2 computers.
   d. 3 computers.

6. If both countries have the same resources, according to the data in Table 2.5, France has an absolute advantage in producing
   a. cheese.   c. both goods.
   b. computers.   d. neither good.

7. According to the data in Table 2.5, the United States has a comparative advantage in producing
   a. cheese.   c. both goods.
   b. computers.   d. neither good.

8. According to the data in Table 2.5, France has a comparative advantage in producing
   a. cheese.
   b. computers.
   c. both goods.
   d. neither good.

9. A production possibility frontier shows maximum production, given
   a. what people want to consume.
   b. rising productivity.
   c. government spending.
   d. the supply of inputs.

Figure 2.3

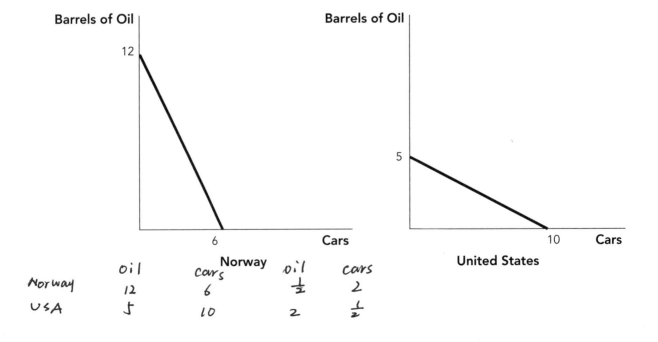

	oil	cars	oil	cars
Norway	12	6	½	2
USA	5	10	2	½

10. In Figure 2.3, the United States has an absolute advantage in producing

    a. oil.

    b. cars.

    c. both oil and cars.

    d. neither oil nor cars.

11. In Figure 2.3, the opportunity cost of oil in Norway is

    a. 0.5 car.

    b. 1 car.

    c. 2 cars.

    d. 6 cars.

12. In Figure 2.3, the opportunity cost of cars in Norway is

    a. 0.5 barrel of oil.

    b. 1 barrel of oil.

    c. 2 barrels of oil.

    d. 10 barrels of oil.

13. In Figure 2.3, the opportunity cost of cars in the United States is

    a. 0.5 barrel of oil.

    b. 1 barrel of oil.

    c. 2 barrels of oil.

    d. 10 barrels of oil.

14. In Figure 2.3, Norway has a comparative advantage in producing

    a. oil.

    b. cars.

    c. both oil and cars.

    d. neither oil nor cars.

15. In Figure 2.3, the United States has a comparative advantage in producing

    a. oil.

    b. cars.

    c. both oil and cars.

    d. neither oil nor cars.

Answers to Self-Practice Questions

1. b, Topic: Trade and Preferences

2. c, Topic: Trade and Preferences

3. d, Topic: Specialization, Productivity, and Division of Knowledge

4. c, Topic: Comparative Advantage

5. a, Topic: Comparative Advantage

6. a, Topic: Comparative Advantage

7. b, Topic: Comparative Advantage

8. a, Topic: Comparative Advantage

9. d, Topic: Comparative Advantage

10. b, Topic: Comparative Advantage

11. a, Topic: Comparative Advantage

12. c, Topic: Comparative Advantage

13. a, Topic: Comparative Advantage

14. a, Topic: Comparative Advantage

15. b, Topic: Comparative Advantage

3

Supply and Demand

Learning Objectives

The objective of this chapter is to learn about demand and supply, using the market for oil as an example. Topics are:

> The Demand Curve for Oil

> The Supply Curve for Oil

According to the authors, as stated in the introduction to this chapter: "Even if you understand little else, you may rightly claim yourself economically literate if you understand these tools. Fail to understand these tools and you will understand little else."

Summary

This chapter covers supply and demand. A **demand curve** is a function that shows the quantity demanded at different prices. As shown in Figure 3.1, **quantity demanded** is the quantity buyers are willing and able to buy at a particular price.

Demand curves are typically downward sloping, implying that if the price falls, the quantity demanded increases. In Figure 3.1, if the price falls from \$10 to \$5, the quantity demanded increases from 100 units to 150 units. Similarly, if the price rises from \$5 to \$10, then the quantity demanded decreases from 150 units to 100 units.

Consumer surplus is the consumer's gain from exchange, or the difference between the maximum price a consumer is willing to pay for a certain good and the market price. For example, if you are willing to pay \$1,000 for a Super Bowl ticket, and the market price is \$480, then your consumer surplus is \$520 = \$1,000 − \$480.

Figure 3.1

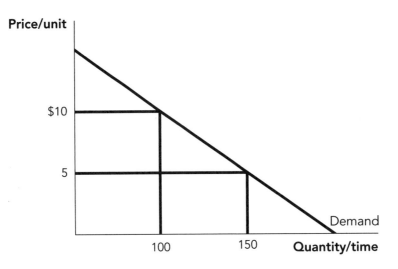

In Figure 3.2, the **total consumer surplus** is measured by the area beneath the demand curve and above the price.

Figure 3.2

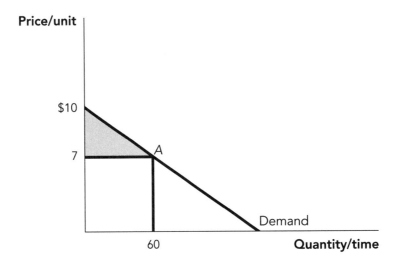

With a market price of $7, the total consumer surplus is the triangle determined by points $7, A, and $10, and it is shaded. The amount of this area can be calculated using the formula for the area of a triangle, which is (height × base)/2. In this example, the height is $3 = $10 − $7 and the base is $60. The height × base is $180 = $3 × $60. The total consumer surplus is $90 = $180/2.

It is important to understand what things cause demand to shift when they change. If, in Figure 3.3, the demand curve shifts from D_1 to D_3, then it is said that demand has increased. This means at every price the quantity of the good that people want to buy is larger. If, in Figure 3.3, the demand curve shifts from D_1 to D_2, it is said that demand has decreased. This means at every price the quantity of the good that people want to buy is smaller.

Among the important things that shift demand are changes in consumer income, population, the price of substitutes and complements, expectations, and tastes (how desirable a good is at a specific point in time).

For some goods, when consumer incomes rise, demand increases. These goods are called **normal goods**. For other goods, when consumer incomes rise, demand decreases. Such goods are called **inferior goods**.

Figure 3.3

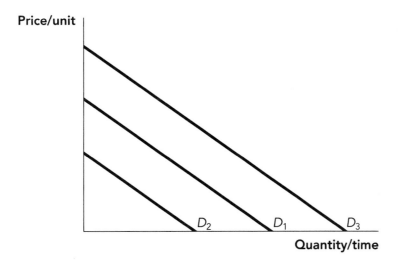

If, when the price of another good goes up and the demand for the original good rises, then the two goods are called **substitutes**. Consumers use one good instead of the other and buy more of the now relatively cheaper of the two goods. If, when the price of another good goes up and the demand for the original good falls, then the two goods are called **complements**. Consumers use the two goods together and buy less of both goods when the price of one of them rises.

If population, tastes (desire) for a good, and the expected future price of the good all increase at the same time, then the demand for the good will also increase. Again, that would be a shift like D_1 to D_3, as shown in Figure 3.3.

A **supply curve** is a function that shows the quantity supplied at different prices. In Figure 3.4, **quantity supplied** is the quantity that sellers are willing to sell at a particular price.

Supply curves are typically upward sloping, implying that if the price rises, then the quantity supplied also increases. In Figure 3.4, if the price rises from $5 to $15, then the quantity supplied increases from 50 units to 200 units. Similarly in Figure 3.4, if the price were to fall from $15 to $5, then the quantity supplied would decrease from 200 units to 50 units.

Figure 3.4

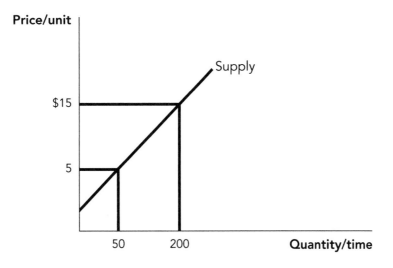

Producer surplus is the producer's gain from exchange, or the difference between the market price and the minimum price at which a producer would be willing to sell a certain quantity. For example, if you are willing to sell your car for $10,000 and the market price is $15,000, then your producer surplus would be $5,000 = $15,000 − $10,000 on that transaction.

Total producer surplus is measured by the area above the supply curve and below the price, as shown in Figure 3.5.

Figure 3.5

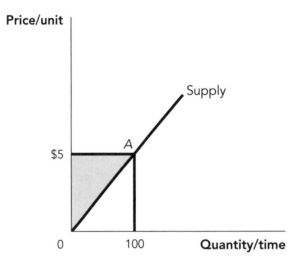

With a market price of $5, the total producer surplus is the triangle determined by points $5, A, and the origin 0,0. Again, the amount of this area can be calculated using the formula for the area of a triangle, which is (height × base)/2. In this example, the height is $5 and the base is 100. The height × base is $500 = $5 × 100. The total consumer surplus is $250 = $500/2.

As with demand, it is important to understand what things will cause supply to shift when they change. If, in Figure 3.6, the supply curve shifts from S_1 to S_3, it is said that supply has increased. This means at every price the quantity of the good that sellers

Figure 3.6

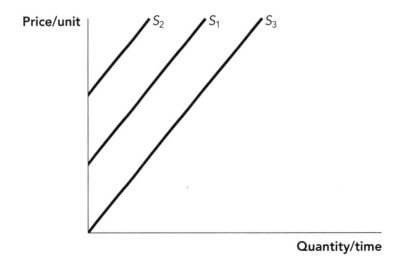

want to sell is larger. If, in Figure 3.6, the supply curve shifts from S_1 to S_2, it is said that supply has decreased. This means at every price the amount of the good that sellers want to sell is smaller.

Among the important things that shift supply are technological change, changes in the price of inputs in production, taxes and subsidies, changes in expectations, entry and exit of producers, and changes in opportunity costs.

If a technology involved in producing calculators improves, then the supply of calculators increases. Similarly, if the price of any input involved in producing calculators falls, then the supply of calculators increases.

If the government taxes the production of calculators, then the supply of calculators decreases. With the tax added, it costs the producer more money to supply calculators. A subsidy is the negative of a tax. If the government subsidizes the production of calculators, then the supply of calculators increases. With the subsidy factored in, it costs the producer less money to produce calculators.

When producers expect a higher price for the product tomorrow (future markets), they have less incentive to sell today (current markets). To the extent that producers can store their product, they will reduce supply today, so they can sell more in the future (when prices are expected to be higher).

An increase in the number of producers also increases supply. For any given amount of supply, if a new producer comes into the market, the supply is increased. Similarly, when any producer leaves the market, this causes a decrease in the amount supplied. In a similar manner, opportunity costs can affect supply. For example, if a self-employed glazier accepts a job installing air-conditioning units that pays more than a job of installing glass and mirrors, then the opportunity cost of installing glass and mirrors has increased. The glazier left the business of glass and mirror installation, thereby reducing supply in that market.

Key Terms

demand curve a function that shows the quantity demanded at different prices

quantity demanded the quantity that buyers are willing and able to buy at a particular price

consumer surplus the consumer's gain from exchange, or the difference between the maximum price a consumer is willing to pay for a certain good and the market price

total consumer surplus the area beneath the demand curve and above the price

normal good a good for which demand increases when income increases

inferior good a good for which demand decreases when income increases

substitutes two goods are substitutes if a decrease in the price of one good leads to a decrease in the demand for the other good

complements two goods are complements if a decrease in the price of one good leads to an increase in the demand for the other good

supply curve a function that shows the quantity supplied at different prices

quantity supplied the quantity that sellers are willing and able to sell at a particular price

producer surplus the producer's gain from exchange, or the difference between the market price and the minimum price at which a producer would be willing to sell a particular quantity

total producer surplus the area above the supply curve and below the price

Traps, Hints, and Reminders

Consumer surplus and producer surplus should not be confused with a surplus on a market. Though these terms have the word "surplus" in them, they are not related to surplus on a market or quantity supplied greater than quantity demanded.

Inferior goods are not necessarily substandard goods. They are simply goods that are negatively related to consumer income. If a person became rich enough, he or she might buy fewer small jets and more custom-fitted commercial jets. This implies that the small jet might be an inferior good to some people at a certain income level, but says nothing about its quality.

Whether goods are complements or substitutes is up to the consumer. To you, butter and margarine may be substitutes, but for the heart patient only margarine is acceptable, and for the pastry chef only butter is usable. You may think of peanut butter and grape jelly as complements; that is, you may only use them together on bread. However, someone else may think of them as substitutes; that is, he may put peanut butter on his toast and not jelly.

On a supply curve, any increase in supply is a shift to the right and down. This can be confusing. With supply or demand, "increase" or "decrease" describes the change along the quantity axis. Thus, an increase in supply is a shift to the right and down, because that moves supply to the right (that is, increasing quantities) along the quantity axis. Similarly, a decrease in supply is a shift up and to the left, because that moves supply to the left (that is, decreasing quantities) along the quantity axis.

A *subsidy* is a negative tax; that is, the government is giving someone money rather than taking it away. You could also think of a tax as a negative subsidy. So quite naturally, taxes and subsidies have opposite effects on supply. Thus, a tax on a product decreases supply, while a subsidy for a product increases supply.

The *area of a triangle* is one-half the height times the base. The area of a triangle can be calculated as $(1/2) \times$ height $\times$ base (or $.5 \times$ height $\times$ base).

Homework Quiz

1. If the price of oil rises, then

    a. the quantity of oil demanded falls. ✓

    b. the demand for oil rises. ↓

    c. the supply of oil rises. ↓

    d. All of the answers are correct.

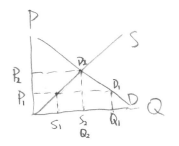

· demand, supply 不看图

· the quantity of demand / supplied 看图

2. A demand curve shows

    a. the maximum willingness to pay for particular quantities.

    b. quantity demanded at different prices.

    c. different combinations of prices and quantities that consumers are able and willing to buy.

    d. All of the answers are correct.

3. If the most Tom is willing to pay for an ice cream cone is $5, and the market price is $2, then by purchasing an ice cream cone, Tom will get a consumer surplus of

    a. $2.

    b. $3.

    c. $5.

    d. $10.

willing − Market price = $5 − $2 = $3

Figure 3.7

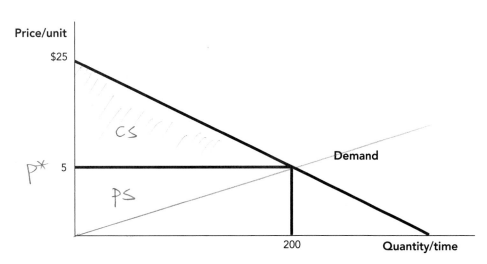

4. In Figure 3.7, if the market price is $5, then total consumer surplus is

    a. $25.

    b. $500.

    c. $1,000.

    d. $2,000.

$25 − 5 = $20

$\dfrac{\$20 \times 200}{2} = \$2000$

过剩的
多余的

5. If consumer incomes rise, then the demand for

    a. inferior goods increases.

    b. normal goods decreases.

    c. inferior goods decreases. 低劣物品

    d. complements decreases. 补充

6. If peanut butter and jelly are complements, then an increase in the price of peanut butter will cause

    a. an increase in the price of jelly.

    b. a decrease in the demand for jelly.

    c. an increase in the demand for peanut butter.

    d. a decrease in the demand for peanut butter.

7. Inferior goods are

    a. substandard. 不够标准的

    b. those with expected future price decreases.

    c. those that are negatively related to consumer income.

    d. those that few people buy.

8. If people's taste for a good goes up due to a fad 短暂的热潮

    a. the current price falls.

    b. the good is a normal good.

    c. the supply of the good decreases.

    d. the demand for the good increases.

9. If the price of oil falls

    a. the supply of oil decreases.

    b. the quantity of oil demanded decreases.

    c. the demand for oil increases.

    d. the quantity of oil supplied decreases.

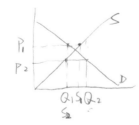

10. Quantity supplied is

    a. negatively related to price.

    b. the amount of a good that sellers are willing and able to sell at a particular price.

    c. price without the willingness to sell.

    d. All of the answers are correct.

11. The difference between the market price and the minimum price at which a producer would be willing to sell a particular quantity is

    a. a demand curve.

    b. a supply curve.

    c. producer surplus.

    d. consumer surplus.

12. In Figure 3.8, an increase in supply is
  a. a move from point *A* to point *B* on S_1.
  b. a move from point *B* to point *A* on S_1.
  c. a shift from S_2 to S_1.
  d. a shift from S_1 to S_2.

Figure 3.8

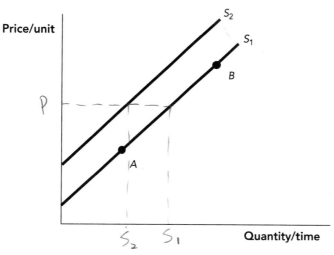

13. If technology increases, the
  a. supply curve decreases.
  b. demand curve decreases.
  c. supply curve increases.
  d. demand curve increases.

supply ↑

14. If firms expect the price of their product to increase in the future
  a. the demand today will decrease.
  b. the price today will decrease.
  c. the price in the future will decrease.
  d. the supply today will decrease.

以后供应 ↑

现在 ↓

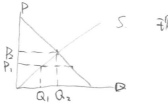

15. If Al's Used Cars sells a car for a market price of $10,000, and the minimum that it would have sold for was $4,000, then the producer surplus of Al's Used Cars is
  a. $4,000.
  b. $6,000.
  c. $10,000.
  d. $40,000.

Market price $10,000 — willing (min).

Self-Practice Questions

1. If the number of buyers of oil rise,

    b

    a. the quantity of oil demanded rises.

    b. the demand for oil rises.   *buyers↑ , Demand ↑*

    c. the supply of oil rises.

    d. All of the answers are correct.

2. Different combinations of prices and quantities that consumers are able and willing to buy is called

    a. a demand curve.

    b. consumer surplus.

    c. a supply curve.

    d. producer surplus.

3. If the most Tom is willing to pay for an ice cream cone is $10, and the market price is $2, then by purchasing an ice cream cone, Tom will get a consumer surplus of

    a. $2.

    b. $8. $p^* 2

    c. $10. $$10 - $2 = 8

    d. $20.

4. If consumer income falls, the demand for

    a. inferior goods decreases.

    b. normal goods decreases.

    c. normal goods increases.

    d. complements decreases.   *替代 ↑↓ ,↓↑*

5. If the price of a substitute for butter rises

    a

    a. the demand for butter increases.

    b. the demand for butter decreases.   *正比 ↑↑,↓↓*

    c. the price of butter falls.

    d. the supply of the substitute decreases.

6. Normal goods are

    a. high quality.

    b. those with expected future price decreases.

    c. those that are positively related to consumer income.

    d. those that most people buy.

7. If the price of oil is expected to fall in the future, the   *以后需求↑*

    a

    a. demand for oil today decreases. ✓

    b. demand for oil in the future decreases.

    c. supply of oil today decreases.

    d. supply of oil in the future increases.

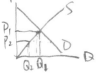

8. If the price of oil rises, the

a. supply of oil decreases.

b. quantity of oil demanded increases.

c. demand for oil increases.

d. quantity of oil supplied increases.

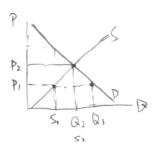

9. Supply is

a. negatively related to price.

b. the amount of a good that sellers are willing and able to sell at a particular price.

c. combinations of quantities and prices that producers are able and willing to sell and sell at, respectively.

d. All of the answers are correct.

10. Producer surplus is

a. the difference between the market price and the minimum price at which a producer would be willing to sell a particular quantity.

b. the difference between the maximum price that a consumer would be willing to pay for a particular quantity and the market price.

c. when the quantity supplied is greater than the quantity demanded.

d. when the quantity demanded is greater than the quantity supplied.

Figure 3.9

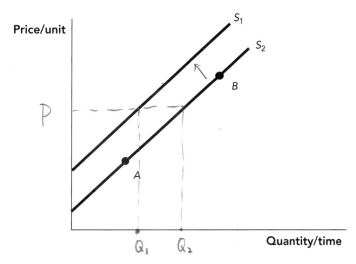

11. In Figure 3.9, a decrease in supply is

a. a move from point A to point B on S_2.

b. a move from point B to point A on S_2.

c. a shift from S_2 to S_1.

d. a shift from S_1 to S_2.

捕入一竹格   工資↑

12. If the price of an input, such as wages of autoworkers, increases, the

a. supply of cars will decrease.

b. supply of cars will increase.

c. price of cars will decrease.

d. supply of autoworkers will decrease.

13. If a firm's opportunity cost of producing a product increases, the supply of that product will

d

a. increase as the number of firms in the industry grows.

b. decrease as the number of firms in the industry grows.

c. increase as the number of firms in the industry falls.

d. decrease as the number of firms in the industry falls.

Figure 3.10

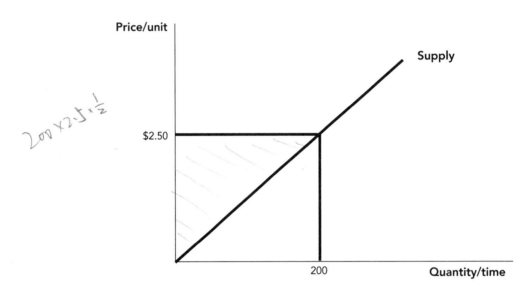

$200 \times 2 \div \frac{1}{2}$

14. In Figure 3.10, total producer surplus is

a. $2.50.

b. $197.50.

c. $250.

d. $500.

15. If the least Tom is willing to sell his 1990 Civic for is $2,000, and the market price is $3,000, then by selling the car, Tom will get producer surplus of

a. $500.

b. $1,000. $3,000 – $2,000

c. $2,000.

d. $5,000.   Ps: MP – willing

Answers to Self-Practice Questions

1. b, Topic: The Demand Curve for Oil

2. a, Topic: The Demand Curve for Oil

3. b, Topic: Consumer Surplus

4. b, Topic: What Shifts the Demand Curve?

5. a, Topic: What Shifts the Demand Curve?

6. c, Topic: What Shifts the Demand Curve?

7. a, Topic: What Shifts the Demand Curve?

8. d, Topic: The Supply Curve for Oil

9. c, Topic: The Supply Curve for Oil

10. a, Topic: Producer Surplus

11. c, Topic: What Shifts the Supply Curve?

12. a, Topic: What Shifts the Supply Curve?

13. d, Topic: What Shifts the Supply Curve?

14. c, Topic: Producer Surplus

15. b, Topic: Producer Surplus

4

Equilibrium: How Supply and Demand Determine Prices

Learning Objectives

In this chapter, demand and supply are again discussed, this time in relation to market equilibrium. Topics included are:

> Equilibrium and the Adjustment Process

> Gains from Trade Are Maximized at the Equilibrium Price and Quantity

> Does the Model Work? Evidence from the Laboratory Shifting Demand and Supply Curves

> Terminology: Demand Compared to Quantity Demanded and Supply Compared to Quantity Supplied

> Understanding the Price of Oil

Summary

The interaction of supply and demand leads to a market equilibrium. As shown in Figure 4.1, market equilibrium occurs where supply and demand intersect.

Figure 4.1

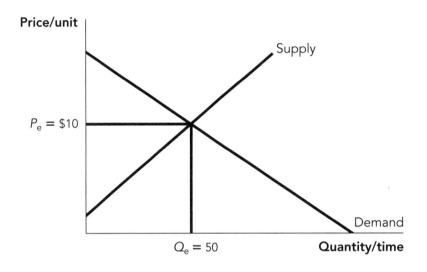

This intersection yields the **equilibrium price**, P_e = $10, and **equilibrium quantity**, Q_e = 50 units of the good.

The market equilibrium is stable, as shown in Figure 4.2, where the equilibrium is still at a price of $10 and a quantity of 50 units.

Figure 4.2

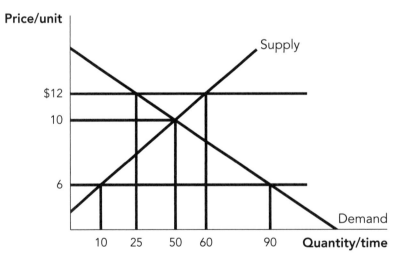

A price of $12 is above equilibrium. At $12, more of the product (60 units) is offered for sale than people want to purchase (25 units). Quantity supplied is greater than quantity demanded by 35 units, implying an excess quantity supplied, or **surplus**.

What will consumers and producers do about the excess quantity supplied? Producers who have rising inventories will start lowering prices below $12. Consumers who see that producers have extra product on hand will start offering prices below $12. Lower prices decrease quantity supplied and increase quantity demanded, moving the market toward equilibrium.

Similarly, a price of $6 is below the equilibrium price. At $6, consumers want to buy more of the product (90 units) than producers want to sell (10 units). This time, quantity demanded is greater than quantity supplied by 80 units, implying an excess quantity demanded, or **shortage**.

What will consumers and producers do about the excess quantity demanded? Consumers, many of whom cannot get the item, will start offering prices above $6. Producers, who see their product flying off the shelf, will start asking prices above $6. Higher prices increase quantity supplied and decrease quantity demanded, again moving the market toward equilibrium.

So whether the price is above or below equilibrium, competitive pressures move price and quantity toward the market equilibrium. Only at the equilibrium does quantity supplied equal quantity demanded, implying no pressure from either consumers or producers to change price.

Gains from trade are maximized at the market equilibrium. This can be seen in Figure 4.3, where the 26th unit is worth slightly less than $12, say $11.99, to the consumer and costs the producer only slightly more than $8, say $8.01.

Figure 4.3

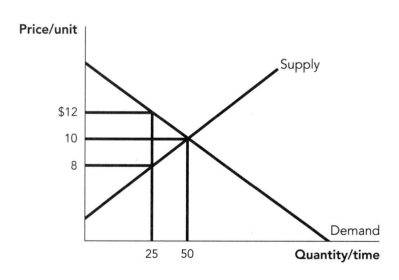

Any price between $11.99 and $8.01 makes both the buyer and seller better off. This is called an unexploited gain from trade. As long as the quantity is below the equilibrium quantity, there will be these unexploited gains from trade.

What if the quantity is above the market equilibrium of 50 units in Figure 4.3? In that case, the cost to producers of producing the unit is greater than what any consumer is willing to pay. So, while consumers are willing to consume the product at some specified price, that price is below the cost of producing the good. Producing such units would waste resources that would be better spent producing something consumers value more.

The free market's maximizing gains from trade means three closely related things. First, the supply of goods is bought by buyers with the highest willingness to pay. Second, the supply of goods is sold by sellers with the lowest costs. Third, between buyers and sellers there are no unexploited gains from trade, or any wasteful trades.

As shown in Figure 4.4, a change in demand causes a movement along the supply curve and a change in quantity supplied.

Figure 4.4

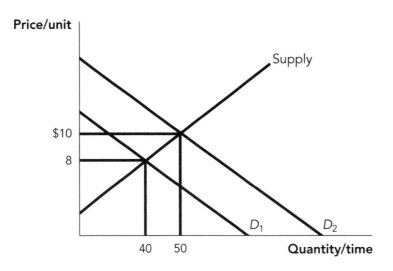

Originally with demand D_1, quantity supplied was 40 units. As demand increased to D_2, quantity moves along the supply curve and quantity supplied becomes 50 units.

For markets with upward-sloping supply curves and downward-sloping demand curves, an increase in demand increases equilibrium price and quantity. As shown in Figure 4.4, the movement of demand from D_1 to D_2 causes the equilibrium price to rise from $8 to $10 and the equilibrium quantity to rise from 40 to 50 units. If demand had decreased from D_2 to D_1, the reverse would have happened. The equilibrium price would have fallen from $10 to $8, and the equilibrium quantity would have fallen from 50 to 40 units.

Similarly, as shown in Figure 4.5, a decrease in supply causes a movement along the demand curve and a change in quantity demanded.

Originally with demand S_1, quantity demanded was 60 units. As supply decreased to D_2, quantity moves along the demand curve and quantity demanded becomes 35 units.

For markets with upward-sloping supply curves and downward-sloping demand curves, a decrease in supply increases equilibrium price and decreases equilibrium quantity. As shown in Figure 4.5, the movement of supply from S_1 to S_2 causes the equilibrium price to rise from $11 to $13 and the equilibrium quantity to fall from 60 to 35 units. If supply had increased from S_2 to S_1, the reverse would have happened. The equilibrium price would have fallen from $13 to $11, and the equilibrium quantity would have risen from 35 to 60 units.

Figure 4.5

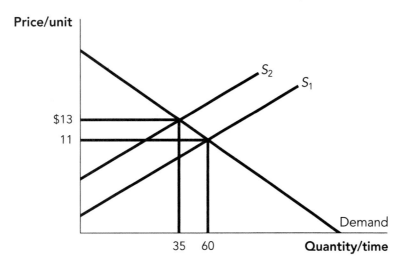

Key Terms

equilibrium price the price at which the quantity demanded is equal to the quantity supplied

equilibrium quantity the quantity at which the quantity demanded is equal to the quantity supplied

surplus a situation in which the quantity supplied is greater than the quantity demanded

shortage a situation in which the quantity demanded is greater than the quantity supplied

Traps, Hints, and Reminders

A surplus should not be confused with consumer or producer surplus, both of which were defined in Chapter 3. A surplus on a market is when quantity supplied is greater than quantity demanded. Consumer surplus is the maximum the consumer is willing to pay less market price. Producer surplus is market price less the minimum price at which the producer would sell.

A free market maximizes the gains from trade, or maximizes producer surplus plus consumer surplus.

A change in demand causes a movement along the supply curve and a change in quantity supplied. Similarly, a change in supply leads to a movement along the demand curve and a change in quantity demanded. The things that can cause changes in quantity demanded or supplied are different from the things that can cause demand and supply to change, as discussed in Chapter 3.

Also recall from Chapter 3 that changes in supply can be somewhat counterintuitive. An increase in supply is a shift to the right and down, while a decrease in supply is a shift up and to the left.

Homework Quiz

1. In an equilibrium market
   a. quantity demanded equals quantity supplied.
   b. total surplus is minimized.
   c. the market price is unstable.
   d. All of the answers are correct.

2. If price is above the equilibrium price, some
   a. consumers will offer to pay a higher price to be sure to get the product.
   b. consumers will offer to pay a lower price because the product is so available.
   c. producers will face excess demand and thus start raising the price.
   d. All of the answers are correct.

3. If price is below the equilibrium price, then
   a. every producer who wants to buy the product can do so.
   b. quantity supplied is greater than quantity demanded. $Q_s < Q_D$
   c. there is a shortage of the product.
   d. All of the answers are correct.

Figure 4.6

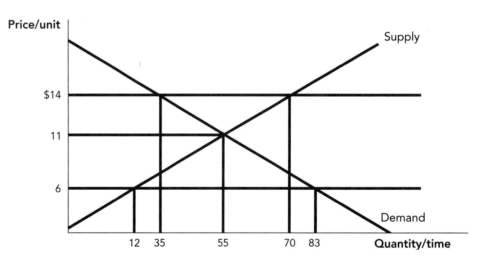

4. In Figure 4.6, the equilibrium price and quantity are
   a. $14 and 70 units.
   b. $11 and 55 units.
   c. $11 and 70 units.
   d. $6 and 12 units.

5. In Figure 4.6, at a price of $14, producers will want to sell
   a. 70 units.
   b. 55 units.
   c. 35 units.
   d. 12 units.

6. In Figure 4.6, at a price of $6, consumers will want to buy

    a. 12 units.

    b. 55 units.

    c. 70 units.

    d. 95 units.

7. In Figure 4.6, at a price of $14, there is an excess quantity

    a. demanded of 83 units.

    b. supplied of 83 units.

    c. demanded of 35 units.

    d. supplied of 35 units.

8. In Figure 4.6, at a price of $6, there is a

    a. shortage of 83 units. $83 - 12 = 71$

    b. surplus of 83 units.

    c. shortage of 35 units.

    d. surplus of 35 units.

9. In a free market equilibrium,

    a. consumer plus producer surplus is maximized.

    b. gains from trade are maximized.

    c. no potential gains from trade are left unexploited.

    d. All of the answers are correct.

10. The free market's maximization of gains from trade implies that

    a. the supply of goods is bought by buyers with the lowest willingness to pay.

    b. the supply of goods is sold by sellers with the lowest costs.

    c. between buyers and sellers there are wasteful trades.

    d. All of the answers are correct.   *any*

11. The free market's maximization of gains from trade implies that

    a. the supply of goods is bought by buyers with the lowest willingness to pay.

    b. the supply of goods is sold by sellers with the highest costs.

    c. there are no unexploited gains from trade, or any wasteful trades, between buyers and sellers.

    d. All of the answers are correct.

Figure 4.7

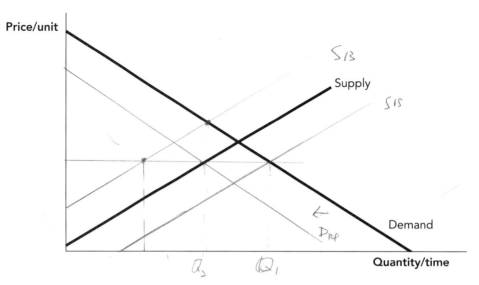

12. In Figure 4.7, if demand increases, then the equilibrium
    a. price and quantity fall.   上移
    b. price and quantity rise.
    c. price falls and quantity rises.
    d. price rises and quantity falls.

13. In Figure 4.7, if supply decreases, then the equilibrium
    a. price and quantity fall.   上移
    b. price and quantity rise.
    c. price falls and quantity rises.
    d. price rises and quantity falls.

14. In Figure 4.7, if the good is normal, and consumer income falls, then the equilibrium   Demand ↓ 下移
    a. price and quantity fall.
    b. price and quantity rise.
    c. price falls and quantity rises.
    d. price rises and quantity falls.

15. In Figure 4.7, if technology improves production of this good, then the equilibrium   Supply ↑, 下移
    a. price and quantity fall.
    b. price and quantity rise.
    c. price falls and quantity rises.
    d. price rises and quantity falls.

Self-Practice Questions

1. If price is above the equilibrium price, some
   a. consumers will offer to pay a higher price to get the product.
   b. producers will sell the product at a higher price.
   c. producers will have excess supplies and thus will start reducing price to get customers.
   d. All of the answers are correct.

2. If price is below the equilibrium price,
   a. every consumer who wants the product can get it.
   b. quantity supplied is greater than quantity demanded for the product. ✗ $Q_s < Q_D$
   c. there is a shortage of the product.
   d. All of the answers are correct.

3. If price is above the equilibrium price,
   a. every producer who wants to sell the product can do so.
   b. quantity supplied is greater than quantity demanded.
   c. there is a shortage of the product. surplus
   d. All of the answers are correct.

Figure 4.8

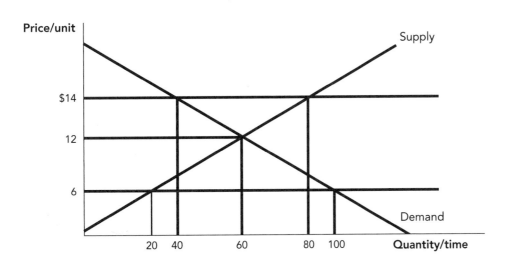

4. In Figure 4.8, the equilibrium price and quantity are
   a. $14 and 100 units.
   b. $12 and 60 units.
   c. $12 and 80 units.
   d. $6 and 40 units.

5. In Figure 4.8, at a price of $14, producers will want to sell
   a. 80 units.
   b. 60 units.
   c. 40 units.
   d. 20 units.

6. In Figure 4.8, at a price of $6, consumers will want to buy
   a. 20 units.
   b. 40 units.
   c. 60 units.
   d. 100 units.

7. In Figure 4.8, at a price of $6, an excess quantity is
   a
   a. demanded of 80 units.   100−20=80
   b. supplied of 80 units.
   c. demanded of 40 units.
   d. supplied of 20 units.

8. In Figure 4.8, at a price of $14, there is a
   d
   a. shortage of 80 units.
   b. surplus of 80 units.
   c. shortage of 40 units.
   d. surplus of 40 units.   80−40=40.

9. The market will NOT produce a quantity greater than equilibrium because
   a. there are unexploited gains from trade still left.
   b. it is illegal.
   c. resources are wasted on production to the right of the equilibrium quantity.
   d. consumer plus producer surplus grows in that region.

10. The free market's maximization of gains from trade implies that
    a. the supply of goods is bought by buyers with the highest willingness to pay.
    b. the supply of goods is sold by sellers with the highest costs.
    c. between buyers and sellers there are unexploited gains from trade.
    d. All of the answers are correct.

Figure 4.9

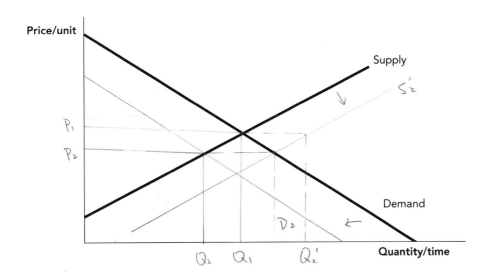

11. In Figure 4.9, if demand decreases, then the equilibrium

    a. price and quantity fall.   下移

    b. price and quantity rise.

    c. price falls and quantity rises.

    d. price rises and quantity falls.

12. In Figure 4.9, if supply increases, then the equilibrium

    a. price and quantity fall.   下移

    b. price and quantity rise.

    c. price falls and quantity rises.

    d. price rises and quantity falls.

13. In Figure 4.9, if the good becomes more popular, then the equilibrium

    a. price and quantity fall.   Demand↑,上移

    b. price and quantity rise.

    c. price falls and quantity rises.

    d. price rises and quantity falls.

14. In Figure 4.9, if the wages of workers producing the good rises, then the equilibrium

    a. price and quantity fall.   工资↑，注supply↓ 上移.

    b. price and quantity rise.

    c. price falls and quantity rises.

    d. price rises and quantity falls.

15. In a free-market equilibrium,

    a. quantity demanded is less than quantity supplied.

    b. the sum of consumer and producer surplus is maximized.

    c. resources are wasted.

    d. there are no exploited gains from trade.

Answers to Self-Practice Questions

1. c, Topic: Equilibrium and the Adjustment Process

2. c, Topic: Equilibrium and the Adjustment Process

3. b, Topic: Equilibrium and the Adjustment Process

4. b, Topic: Equilibrium and the Adjustment Process

5. a, Topic: Equilibrium and the Adjustment Process

6. d, Topic: Equilibrium and the Adjustment Process

7. a, Topic: Equilibrium and the Adjustment Process

8. d, Topic: Gains from Trade Are Maximized at the Equilibrium

9. c, Topic: Shifting Demand and Supply

10. a, Topic: Shifting Demand and Supply

11. a, Topic: Shifting Demand and Supply

12. c, Topic: Shifting Demand and Supply

13. b, Topic: Shifting Demand and Supply

14. d, Topic: Shifting Demand and Supply

15. b, Topic: Terminology

5

Elasticity and Its Applications

Learning Objectives

In this chapter, the authors introduce the concept of elasticity, which allows us to discuss demand in practical terms. The topics to be learned include:

> The Elasticity of Demand
> The Elasticity of Supply
> Using Elasticities for Quick Predictions (Optional)
> Appendix 1: Using Excel to Calculate Elasticities
> Appendix 2: Other Types of Elasticities

Summary

Elasticity allows us to move from the theory of supply and demand to practical applications. Elasticity asks the questions—how much quantity is demanded or how much does supply change when something else changes?

Elasticity of demand measures how sensitive the quantity demanded is to a change in price. If the quantity demanded is very sensitive to a change in price, we call it elastic. If the quantity demanded is not very sensitive to a change in price, we call it inelastic.

As shown in Figure 5.1, a relatively flat demand curve is more elastic than a steeper demand curve at any given point. For a $1 price increase, the quantity demanded falls 6 units on the elastic; that is, there is a more responsive demand curve. For the same $1 price increase, the quantity demanded falls only 1 unit on the inelastic; that is, there is a relatively less responsive demand curve.

Figure 5.1

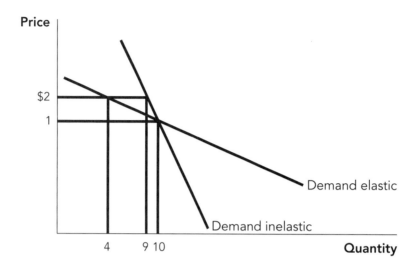

Goods that have fewer substitutes, are necessities, are categories of goods, and comprise a smaller part of consumers' budgets have more inelastic demands. Goods that have more substitutes are luxuries, are specific brands, and comprise a larger part of consumers' budgets have more elastic demands. The demand for any good is more inelastic in a shorter time frame than in a longer time frame.

Elasticity of demand is calculated as the percentage change in quantity demanded divided by the percentage change in price.

$$\text{Elasticity of demand} = E_D = \frac{\text{Percentage Change in Quantity Demanded}}{\text{Percentage Change in Price}}$$

$$= \frac{\% \Delta Q_{demanded}}{\% \Delta Price}$$

The symbol delta, Δ, means change, and the resulting negative number is taken in absolute terms; that is, it is taken to be positive. Thus, if the percentage change in price is 50 percent and the percentage change in quantity demanded is 100 percent, then the elasticity of demand = (100%/50%) = 2. Also, if the percentage change price is 50 percent and the percentage change in quantity demanded is 25 percent, then the elasticity of demand = (25%/50%) = 0.5 (or ½). Note that in these demand elasticity examples, either the percentage change in price or the percentage change in quantity must be negative. We are dropping the sign or taking the absolute values in our calculations.

Anytime the percentage change in quantity demanded is greater than the percentage change in price, the elasticity of demand will be greater than 1 and is therefore called elastic. Anytime the percentage change in quantity demanded is less than the percentage change in price, the elasticity of demand will be less than 1 and is therefore called inelastic. In the special case in which the percentage change in quantity equals the percentage change in price, the elasticity of demand equals 1 and it is called unit elastic.

Elasticity also indicates the relationship between price and total revenue from selling the good. Total revenue is the price multiplied by the quantity. When demand is elastic, price and total revenue move in opposite directions. This is because when price goes up a little, the quantity demanded goes down a lot. As a result, total revenue declines because the price increase is more than offset by the decrease in the quantity demanded. When demand is inelastic, price and total revenue move in the same direction. This is because when price goes up a lot, the quantity demanded goes down only a little. Thus, total revenue rises since the price increase is not completely offset by the decrease in the quantity demanded. In the case when demand is unit elastic, as price goes up, the quantity demanded goes down by the same proportion, and thus total revenue is unchanged. In other words, with unit elasticity, price and total revenue are unrelated because when price changes total revenue does not.

Consider the points on the demand curves we called elastic and inelastic in Figure 5.1. Total revenue is initially 1×10 units $= \$10$. When price rises to $2 on the relatively elastic demand curve, the quantity demanded falls to 4 units. Thus, total revenue becomes 2×4 units $= \$8$ and, as price rises on the relatively elastic demand curve, total revenue falls. When price rises to $2 on the relatively inelastic demand curve, the quantity demanded falls to 9 units. Thus, total revenue becomes 2×9 units $= \$18$ and, as price rises on the relatively inelastic demand curve, total revenue rise.

Of course the reverse is also true in each case. If price falls, then total revenue on an inelastic demand curve falls. If price falls, then total revenue rises on an elastic demand curve. The relationship between elasticity of demand and total revenue is summarized in the following table.

Absolute Value of Elasticity	Name	Price and Total Revenue
$E_D < 1$	Inelastic	move together
$E_D > 1$	Elastic	move opposite directions
$E_D = 1$	Unit Elastic	are unrelated

Elasticity of supply measures how sensitive the quantity supplied is to a change in price. As with elasticity of demand, a steeper supply curve is relatively more inelastic while a flatter supply curve is relatively more elastic.

Two extreme cases of elasticity of supply are shown in Figure 5.2.

In Figure 5.2, supply (as shown in the left graph) is perfectly elastic. In this case, price does not change when the quantity demanded changes. In Figure 5.2, supply (as shown in the right graph) is perfectly inelastic. In this case, quantity demanded does not change when price changes.

Supply is less elastic when it is difficult to increase production at unit costs; production uses up a large share of the market for inputs, for global supply, and in the

Figure 5.2

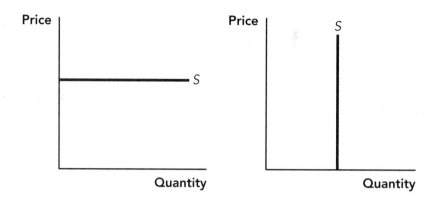

short run. Supply is more elastic when it is easy to increase production at unit costs; production uses up a small share of the market for inputs, for local supply, and in the long run.

Elasticity of supply is also calculated as percentage change in the quantity supplied divided by the percentage change in price, where delta, Δ, still means change.

$$\text{Elasticity of supply} = E_S = \frac{\text{Percentage Change in Quantity Supplied}}{\text{Percentage change in Price}}$$

$$= \frac{\% \Delta Q_{Supplied}}{\% \Delta Price}$$

The resulting value is positive for the elasticity of supply, because when the price increases, so does the quantity. Thus, if the percentage change in price is 100 percent and the percentage change in the quantity supplied is 300 percent, then elasticity of supply = (300%/100%) = 3. Also, if the percentage change in price is 80 percent and the percentage change in the quantity supplied is 20 percent, then the elasticity of supply = (20%/80%) = ¼ (or 0.25).

Elasticities can be used to predict changes in price from demand or supply shifts. If demand increases by 10 percent, the elasticity of demand, E_D, is ½ (or 0.5), and the elasticity of supply, E_S, is 2, then these numbers can be plugged into the following formula:

$$\text{Percentage change in Price from a shift in supply} = \frac{\text{Percentage Change in Supply}}{(E_D + E_S)}$$

Using these numbers would give 10/(2 + ½) or (10/2.5) = 4. Thus, in this example, we predict a 4 percent increase in price.

Similar formulas can be used to predict percentage change in price from a supply shift and percentage change in quantity from either a supply or a demand shift, for instance:

$$\text{Percentage change in Price from a shift in supply} = -\frac{\text{Percentage Change in Supply}}{(E_D + E_S)}$$

Notice the equation above has a minus sign in front of the right side.

Percentage change in Quantity from a shift in demand

$$= E_S \times \frac{(\text{Percentage Change in Demand})}{(E_D + E_S)}$$

Percentage change in Quantity from a shift in supply

$$= E_D \times \frac{(\text{Percentage Change in Supply})}{(E_D + E_S)}$$

Appendix 1: Using Excel to Calculate Elasticities

Percentage changes depend on one's point of reference. Thus, we calculate elastiticities along a range of points based on the midpoint of the change. This is shown in the following formula:

$$\text{Elasticity of demand} = E_D = \frac{\dfrac{\text{Change in Quantity Demanded}}{\text{Average Quantity}}}{\dfrac{\text{Change in Price}}{\text{Average Price}}}$$

$$= \frac{\dfrac{Q_{before} - Q_{after}}{(Q_{before} + Q_{after})/2}}{\dfrac{P_{before} - P_{after}}{(P_{before} + P_{after})/2}}$$

For example, if at \$3 people buy 100 units of a product, and at \$1 people buy 200 units of a product, then:

$$E_D = \frac{\dfrac{Q_{before} - Q_{after}}{(Q_{before} + Q_{after})/2}}{\dfrac{P_{before} - P_{after}}{(P_{before} + P_{after})/2}} = \frac{\dfrac{100 - 200}{(100 + 200)/2}}{\dfrac{\$3 - \$1}{(\$3 + \$1)/2}} = \frac{\dfrac{100}{150}}{\dfrac{1}{1}} = 2/3 \text{ (or } 0.67)$$

Notice that we have dropped the minus sign. Also notice, as expected with a calculated elasticity of less than one, that when the price fell from \$3 to \$1, the total revenue also fell from \$300 to \$200.

A similar formula allows calculation of elasticity of supply over a range of points.

$$\text{Elasticity of supply} = E_S = \frac{\dfrac{\text{Change in Quantity Supplied}}{\text{Average Quantity}}}{\dfrac{\text{Change in Price}}{\text{Average Price}}}$$

$$= \frac{\dfrac{Q_{\text{before}} - Q_{\text{after}}}{(Q_{\text{before}} + Q_{\text{after}})/2}}{\dfrac{P_{\text{before}} - P_{\text{after}}}{(P_{\text{before}} + P_{\text{after}})/2}}$$

Appendix 2: Other Types of Elasticities

One can compute elasticities between any two variables that are related. Two other important variables are cross-price elasticity of demand and income elasticity.

Cross-price elasticity measures how sensitive the quantity demanded for one good is to the price of another good. It is calculated using the following formula, where delta, Δ, still means change.

Cross-Price Elasticity of demand Good A

$$= \frac{\text{Percentage Change in Quantity Demanded of Good A}}{\text{Percentage Change in Price of Good B}}$$

$$= \frac{\%\Delta Q_{\text{demanded of Good A}}}{\%\Delta \text{ Price of Good B}}$$

Or, if you have data on two different prices of good B, you would use the following midpoint formula for cross-price elasticity.

$$\frac{\dfrac{\text{Change in Quantity Demanded A}}{\text{Average Quantity of Good A}}}{\dfrac{\text{Change in Price B}}{\text{Average Price of Good B}}} = \frac{\dfrac{Q_{\text{before A}} - Q_{\text{after A}}}{(Q_{\text{before A}} + Q_{\text{after A}})/2}}{\dfrac{P_{\text{before B}} - P_{\text{after B}}}{(P_{\text{before B}} + P_{\text{after B}})/2}}$$

If the cross-price elasticity is > 0, then goods A and B are substitutes. If the cross-price elasticity is < 0, then goods A and B are complements.

Income elasticity measures how sensitive the quantity demanded of a good is to changes in consumer income. It is calculated using the following formula, in which delta, Δ, still stands for change.

$$\text{Income Elasticity of demand} = \frac{\text{Percentage Change in Quantity Demanded}}{\text{Percentage Change in Income}}$$

$$= \frac{\%\Delta Q_{\text{demanded}}}{\%\Delta \text{Income}}$$

Or, if you have data on two different consumer income levels, you would use the midpoint formula for income elasticity.

$$\frac{\dfrac{\text{Change in Quantity Demanded}}{\text{Average Quantity}}}{\dfrac{\text{Change in Income}}{\text{Average Income}}} = \frac{\dfrac{Q_{\text{before}} - Q_{\text{after}}}{(Q_{\text{before}} + Q_{\text{after}})/2}}{\dfrac{I_{\text{before}} - I_{\text{after}}}{(I_{\text{before}} + I_{\text{after}})/2}}$$

If the income elasticity is > 0, then the good is a normal good. If the income elasticity is < 0, then the good is inferior. Some economists define cases in which income elasticity of demand is > 1 as luxury goods.

Key Terms

elasticity of demand a measure of how responsive the quantity demanded is to a change in price

elasticity of supply a measure of how responsive the quantity supplied is to a change in price

Traps, Hints, and Reminders

Remember, with elasticity of demand take the absolute value or drop the sign. The meanings of elasticity of demand are all in terms of positive values.

All of the elasticities in this chapter follow one general formula: Percentage change in quantity demanded or supplied is divided by percentage change in some other variable. The variable is in the denominator (i.e., on the bottom)—demand price, supply price, the cross-price, or price of another good or income—and gives the name to the elasticity (such as demand elasticity, supply elasticity, cross-price elasticity, or income elasticity).

When thinking about the relationship of price and total revenue, think of a string or even a steel rod if you like. A string or steel rod is relatively inelastic. If price and total revenue were tied together with a string or hooked together by a steel rod, then when price rises, total revenue also rises, and when price falls, total revenue also falls.

If you have data on two "price and quantity demanded" combinations, you can partly check your calculated elasticity of demand by checking to see if the relationship between price and total revenue is as it should be. For example, if you calculate a demand elasticity of ½ (or 0.5), but discover that as price goes up in your data, total revenue goes down, you should know that you must have made a calculation error someplace. Thus, you should recheck your calculations.

An increase in supply decreases price such that the predicted change in price, from a shift in supply, has a negative sign in front of the formula.

Homework Quiz

1. A demand curve that is relatively responsive to price changes is
   a. more elastic.
   b. more inelastic.
   c. perfectly inelastic.
   d. more inferior.

2. A supply curve that is relatively unresponsive to price changes is
   a. more elastic.
   b. more inelastic.
   c. perfectly elastic.
   d. less inferior.

3. Elasticity of demand measures the
   a. responsiveness of price to a change in the quantity demanded.
   b. responsiveness of price to a change in the quantity supplied.
   c. responsiveness of the quantity demanded to a change in price.
   d. responsiveness of the quantity supplied to a change in price.

4. Elasticity of supply measures the
   a. responsiveness of price to a change in the quantity demanded.
   b. responsiveness of price to a change in the quantity supplied.
   c. responsiveness of the quantity demanded to a change in price.
   d. responsiveness of the quantity supplied to a change in price.

5. A flatter supply curve is relatively more elastic than a steeper supply curve because
   a. price changes relatively more than the quantity supplied.
   b. the quantity supplied changes relatively more than price.
   c. the quantity demanded changes more than the quantity supplied.
   d. the quantity supplied is relatively insensitive to price changes.

6. A perfectly elastic supply curve is
   a. downward sloping.
   b. upward sloping.
   c. horizontal. //
   d. vertical. ⊥

7. If the absolute value of elasticity of demand is 0.25 (or 1/4), then

    a. demand is elastic.

    b. the quantity demanded is relatively insensitive to price changes.

    c. when price rises, total revenue falls.

    d. All of the answers are correct.

$E_D < 1$, Inelasticity

8. If elasticity of demand is 2.5, then

    a. demand is elastic. $E > 1$, elastic.

    b. price and total revenue move in the opposite directions. ✓

    c. the quantity demanded is relatively sensitive to price changes. ✓

    d. All of the answers are correct.

9. If elasticity of demand is unit elastic, then

    a. price and total revenue move together.

    b. demand is elastic.

    c. total revenue does not change when price changes.

    d. All of the answers are correct.

10. Supply will be more elastic (local supply) long run

    a. in a longer time frame.

    b. for raw materials.

    c. for global supply. (less elastic) short run

    d. All of the answers are correct.

11. Demand will be more inelastic

    a. in the short run. ✓

    b. if the good is a small percentage of the consumer's budget. ✓

    c. if the good has few substitutes.

    d. All of the answers are correct.

12. If when price rises by 5 percent, the quantity demanded falls by 10 percent, then the absolute value of elasticity of demand is

    a. 0.5 (or 1/2).

    b. 2.

    c. 15.

    d. 50.

$\frac{\Delta Q}{\Delta P} = \frac{10\%}{5\%} = 2$

13. If when price rises by 200 percent, the quantity supplied increases by 50, then the elasticity of supply is

a. 0.25 (or 1/4).

$$\frac{\partial Q_s}{\partial P} = \frac{50\%}{200\%} = \frac{1}{4} = 25\%$$

b. 4.

c. 250.

d. 10,000.

14. The absolute value of the elasticity of demand for gasoline is 0.5 (or 1/2) and the elasticity of supply is 1.5 (or 3/2). If demand increases by 10 percent, then you would expect the price of gasoline to rise by

a. 2 percent.

$$\frac{10}{20} = \frac{1}{2} \qquad \frac{3}{2}$$

b. 5 percent.

c. 10 percent.

d. None of the answers is correct.

15. The elasticity of demand for cars is 0.2 and the elasticity of supply is 0.8. If supply increases by 15 percent, then you would expect the price of cars to fall by

a. 1 percent.

$$\frac{2}{10} \qquad \frac{8}{10} \wedge \frac{15}{}$$

b. 4.33 percent.

c. 15 percent.

d. None of the answers is correct.

Appendixes

16. If the income elasticity is negative, then the good is

a. elastic.

b. inelastic.

c. inferior.

d. normal.

17. Suppose that when peanut butter is $5, firms supply 2,000 units, and when peanut butter is $1, firms supply 1,000 units. Using the midpoint formula, the elasticity of supply for peanut butter is

$$\frac{\frac{1000}{1500}}{\frac{4}{2}} = \frac{\frac{10}{15}\cdot\frac{3}{4}}{} = \frac{1}{2}$$

a. 0 (zero).

b. 0.5 (1/2).

c. 1.

d. 2.

Self-Practice Questions

1. A demand curve that is relatively unresponsive to price changes is
   a. more elastic.
   b. more inelastic.
   c. perfectly inelastic.
   d. more inferior.

2. A supply curve that is relatively responsive to price changes is
   a. more elastic.
   b. more inelastic.
   c. perfectly elastic.
   d. less inferior.

3. Elasticity of demand measures the responsiveness of
   a. price to a change in the quantity demanded.
   b. price to a change in the quantity supplied.
   c. the quantity demanded to a change in price.
   d. the quantity supplied to a change in price.

4. Elasticity of supply measures the responsiveness of
   a. price to a change in the quantity demanded.
   b. price to a change in the quantity supplied.
   c. the quantity demanded to a change in price.
   d. the quantity supplied to a change in price.

5. A steeper demand curve is relatively less elastic than a flatter demand curve because
   a. price changes relatively more than the quantity supplied.
   b. the quantity demanded changes relatively more than price.
   c. the quantity demanded changes more than the quantity supplied.
   d. the quantity demanded is relatively sensitive to price changes.

6. A perfectly inelastic supply curve is
   a. downward sloping.
   b. upward sloping.
   c. horizontal.
   d. vertical.

7. If the absolute value of elasticity of demand is 0.5 (or 1/2), then

b

a. demand is elastic. X $\varepsilon < 1$, Inelasticity

b. the quantity demanded is relatively <u>insensitive</u> to price changes. x

c. when price rises, total revenue falls.

d. All of the answers are correct.

8. If elasticity of demand is 3.0, then

a. demand is elastic.

b. price and total revenue move in the opposite directions.

c. the quantity demanded is relatively sensitive to price changes.

d. All of the answers are correct.

9. If elasticity of demand is (unit) elastic, then

C

a. price and total revenue move together. X

b. demand is elastic. ✓

c. total revenue and price are unrelated. X

d. All of the answers are correct.

10. Supply will be less elastic

a. in a longer time frame.

b. for a small share of the market for inputs.

c. for global supply.

d. All of the answers are correct.

11. Demand will be more elastic

a. in the short run. X long

b. if the good is a small percentage of the consumer's budget. large

c. if the good has many substitutes. ✓

d. All of the answers are correct.

12. Suppose that when price rises by 20 percent, the quantity demanded falls by 10 percent. Then the absolute value of elasticity of demand is

a. 0.5 (or 1/2). $\frac{\Delta Q}{\Delta P} = \frac{10\%}{20\%} = \frac{1}{2}$

b. 2.

c. 30.

d. 200.

13. Suppose that when price rises by 20 percent, the quantity supplied increases by 80 percent. Then the elasticity of supply is

a. 0.25 (or 1/4).

b. 4.

c. 100.

d. 1,600.

$$\frac{\Delta Q}{\Delta P} = \frac{80\%}{20\%} = 4$$

14. Suppose that the absolute value of the elasticity of demand for gasoline is 0.5 (or 1/2), and the elasticity of supply is 0.5 (or 1/2). If demand increases 10 percent, then you would expect the price of gasoline to rise by

a. 2 percent.

b. 5 percent.

c. 10 percent.

d. None of the answers is correct.

15. Suppose that the elasticity of demand for cars is 0.2, and the elasticity of supply is 0.8. If supply increases 10 percent, then you would expect the price of cars to fall by

b

a. 1 percent.

b. 10 percent.

c. 20 percent.

d. None of the answers is correct.

Appendixes

16. If cross-price elasticity is positive, then the two goods are

a. substitutes.

b. inferior.

c. normal.

d. complements.

17. Suppose that when the price of butter is $1, consumers buy 100 units of margarine, and when the price of butter is $3, consumers buy 900 units of margarine. Then the cross-price elasticity between butter and margarine is

a. −3.2.

b. −1.6.

c. 1.6.

d. 3.2.

$$\frac{\frac{800}{500}}{\frac{2}{2}} = \frac{8}{5}$$

Answers to Self-Practice Questions

1. b, Topic: Elasticity of Demand

2. a, Topic: Elasticity of Supply

3. c, Topic: Elasticity of Demand

4. d, Topic: Elasticity of Supply

5. d, Topic: Elasticity of Demand

6. d, Topic: Elasticity of Supply

7. b, Topic: Elasticity of Demand

8. d, Topic: Elasticity of Demand

9. c, Topic: Elasticity of Demand

10. c, Topic: Elasticity of Supply

11. c, Topic: Elasticity of Demand

12. a, Topic: Elasticity of Demand

13. b, Topic: Elasticity of Supply

14. c, Topic: Using Elasticities for Quick Predictions

15. b, Topic: Using Elasticities for Quick Predictions

16. a, Topic: Other Types of Elasticities

17. c, Topic: Other Types of Elasticities

6

Taxes and Subsidies

Learning Objectives

In Chapter 3 we learned briefly how taxes and subsidies cause supply to shift. Here they are discussed in more detail. Topics covered are:

> Commodity Taxes

> Subsidies

We also examine who pays a tax or gets a subsidy.

Summary

Deadweight losses and lost gains from trade can be caused by a commodity tax on a market, as can be seen from Figure 6.1, where a $5 per unit tax is imposed on the market.

The pre-tax equilibrium was a price of $12 and a quantity exchanged of 100 units. Notice that pre-tax, consumer surplus is the area $A + B + C + E$, producer surplus is the area $F + G + H$, and total surplus is $A + B + C + E + F + G + H$.

After the tax, the new equilibrium price of $15 is paid by the consumers and the new equilibrium quantity is 90 units. Additionally since $5 of that $15 price must be paid to the government in the form of a tax, the post-tax price received by sellers is $10. Thus, the tax per unit is the amount paid by consumers, $15, less the amount received by sellers, $10, or $15 − $10 = $5, as originally specified. The tax is sometimes called a wedge between what the buyer pays and the seller receives for the product.

Notice also that the amount of exchange fell. The reason people were buying and firms were selling the units between 90 and 100 is because they gained from buying and selling them. Thus, by reducing exchange, the tax creates a deadweight loss of area $E + G$.

Figure 6.1

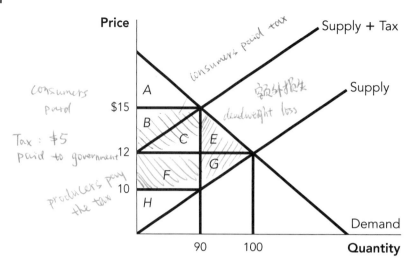

The amount of the tax is the vertical distance between the two supply curves, $5 in this example, and it is paid on the equilibrium quantity exchanged post-tax of 90 units. Thus, the amount of tax paid is $450, or area *B* + *C* + *F*. Consumers pay the difference between the original equilibrium price and the post-tax equilibrium price, $15 − $12, or $3 times the 90 units, which is $270 of the tax, or area *B* + *C*. Producers pay the other part of the tax $450 − $270, or $2 × 90 units, both of which equal $180, or area *F*.

We can also see the deadweight loss or lost gains from trade by comparing the pre-tax total surplus area *A* + *B* + *C* + *E* + *F* + *G* + *H* to the post-tax situation. Post-tax consumer surplus is area *A*, producer surplus is area *H*, and the amount of the tax paid is area *B* + *C* + *F*. That means post-tax total surplus is *A* + *B* + *C* + *F* + *H*. Pre-tax total surplus (*A* + *B* + *C* + *E* + *F* + *G* + *H*) less post-tax total surplus (*A* + *B* + *C* + *F* + *H*) gives the deadweight loss of *E* + *G*.

This also illustrates two other points about commodity taxes. The first point is that who pays the tax does not depend on who writes the check to the government. In our example, the $5 commodity tax was imposed on producers, yet even though they wrote the $450 check to the government they paid less than half the tax, $180. Had we modeled the $5 tax as a tax on demanders in this exact same market we would have come to exactly the same new equilibrium price and quantity of $15 and 90 units. We would also have the exact same distribution of the burden of the tax, $270, paid by consumers, and $180, paid by producers.

The second point is that who pays the tax depends on relative elasticities of supply and demand. The general rule is the less elastic side of the market pays more of the tax. Thus, in Figure 6.1, supply must be slightly more elastic than demand as demanders paid slightly more of the tax.

A subsidy is the negative of a tax. Rather than taking money from someone, as a tax does, with a subsidy the government gives someone money. Thus, a subsidy is very similar to a tax.

Who gets the subsidy does not depend on who receives the check from the government. Who benefits from the subsidy does depend on the relative elasticities of demand and supply. Subsidies must be paid for by taxpayers, and they create deadweight losses by increasing exchange beyond the unsubsidized equilibrium and causing resources to be wasted.

A minimum wage raises wages but reduces exchange in the market and thus decreases employment of low-wage workers. A low-wage subsidy would raise wages and increase the exchange in the low-wage-worker market and thus increase the employment of low wage workers. For this reason some economists prefer a low-wage subsidy to a minimum wage, if the government is going to interfere in the low-wage labor market.

Key Terms

tax wedge the price paid by buyers less the price received by sellers

subsidy wedge the price received by sellers less the price paid by buyers.

Traps, Hints, and Reminders

A subsidy is just the negative or the opposite of a tax. In the case of a tax, the government is making people pay taxes and receiving the money. In the case of a subsidy, the government is giving people money and taxpayers must pay for this.

With a tax, the consumer pays the difference between the old price and the new price on each unit.

With a tax, the part of the tax not paid by consumers is paid by sellers or producers.

Homewor Quiz

1. With a commodity subsidy *does not*
   a. who benefits depends on who gets the check from the government.
   b. who benefits depends on the relative elasticities of supply and demand.
   c. there are no deadweight losses.
   d. All of the answers are correct.

Figure 6.2

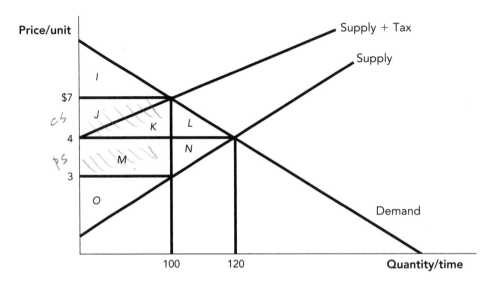

2. In Figure 6.2, the price the consumer pays for the product after the commodity tax is
   a. $3.
   b. $4.
   c. $7.
   d. None of the answers is correct.

3. In Figure 6.2, the price the producer receives for the product after the commodity tax is
   a. $3.
   b. $4.
   c. $7.
   d. None of the answers is correct.

4. In Figure 6.2, the government tax revenue with the commodity tax is area
   a. *J* + *K* + *M*.
   b. *L* + *N*.
   c. *J* + *K*.
   d. *M*.

5. In Figure 6.2, the government tax revenue with the commodity tax is

a. $100.

b. $300.

c. $400.

d. None of the answers is correct.

$(7-3)\ 100 \ = 4 \times 100 = \$400$

6. In Figure 6.2, the part of the commodity tax paid by consumers is area

a. $J + K + M.$

b. $L + N.$

c. $J + K.$

d. $M.$

7. In Figure 6.2, the part of the commodity tax paid by consumers is

a. $100.

b. $300.

c. $400.

d. None of the answers is correct.

8. In Figure 6.2, the part of the commodity tax paid by producers is area

a. $J + K + M.$

b. $L + N.$

c. $J + K.$

d. $M.$

9. In Figure 6.2, the part of the commodity tax paid by producers is

a. $100.

b. $300.

c. $400.

d. None of the answers is correct.

10. In Figure 6.2, the deadweight loss due to the commodity tax is area

a. $J + K + M.$

b. $L + N.$

c. $J + K.$

d. $M.$

11. If the elasticity of supply of water is less than the elasticity of demand for water, then the benefits of a per unit subsidy of water would

a. be split roughly evenly between buyers and sellers.

b. go mainly to buyers.

c. go mainly to sellers.

d. go mainly to the government.

D for food is more E

who is inelasticity?

benefit: sellers, because is inelasticity part.

12. A low-wage subsidy

    a. raises low-wage worker employment and wages.

    b. lowers low-wage worker employment and wages.

    c. raises low-wage worker wages, while employment falls.

    d. lowers low-wage worker wages, while employment rises.

13. With a commodity subsidy,

    a. who benefits does not depend on who gets the check from the government.

    b. the consumer always gets all of the subsidy.

    c. there are no deadweight losses.

    d. All of the answers are correct.

14. With a commodity subsidy, *does not*

    a. who benefits depends on who gets the check from the government.

    b. the producer always gets all of the subsidy.

    c. there are deadweight losses.

    d. All of the answers are correct.

15. With a commodity tax,

    a. who pays the tax does not depend on who writes the check to the government.

    b. who pays the tax depends on the relative elasticities of supply and demand.

    c. the government gets revenue, and the tax causes deadweight losses.

    d. All of the answers are correct.

Self-Practice Questions

1. With a commodity tax,

    a. who pays the tax does not depend on who writes the check to the government.

    b. who pays the tax depends on the relative elasticities of supply and demand.

    c. the government gets revenue, and the tax causes deadweight losses.

    d. All of the answers are correct.

Figure 6.3

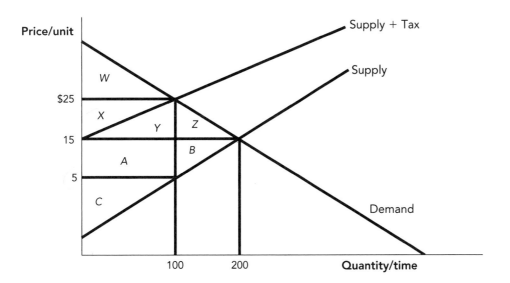

2. In Figure 6.3, the price the consumer pays for the product after the commodity tax is
   a. $5.
   b. $15.
   c. $25.
   d. None of these answers is correct.

3. In Figure 6.3, the price the producer receives for the product after the commodity tax is
   a. $5.
   b. $15.
   c. $25.
   d. None of the answers is correct.

4. In Figure 6.3, government tax revenue with the commodity tax is area
   a. $X + Y + A$.
   b. $X + Y$.
   c. A.
   d. $Z + B$.

5. In Figure 6.3, the government tax revenue with the commodity tax is
   a. $100. $(25-5) \times 100$
   b. $1,000.
   c. $2,000.
   d. None of the answers is correct.

6. In Figure 6.3, the part of the commodity tax paid by consumers is area

a. $X + Y + A.$

b. $X + Y.$

c. $A.$

d. $Z + B.$

7. In Figure 6.3, the part of the commodity tax paid by consumers is

a. $100.

b. $1,000.

c. $2,000.

d. None of the answers is correct.

8. In Figure 6.3, the part of the commodity tax paid by producers is area

a. $X + Y + A.$

b. $X + Y.$

c. $A.$

d. $Z + B.$

9. In Figure 6.3, the part of the commodity tax paid by producers is

a. $100.

b. $1,000.

c. $2,000.

d. None of the answers is correct.

10. In Figure 6.3, the deadweight loss due to the commodity tax is area

a. $X + Y.$

b. $Z + A.$

c. $A + C.$

d. $Z + B.$

11. If the elasticity of supply of pizza is more than the elasticity of demand for pizza, then the cost of a per unit tax on pizza would

a. be split roughly evenly between buyers and sellers.

b. fall mainly on buyers.

c. fall mainly on sellers.

d. fall mainly on the government.

12. A low-wage subsidy:

a. increases total surplus.

b. lowers employment.

c. puts a wedge between wages paid by firms and their employees.

d. All these answers are correct.

13. With a commodity tax,

    a. who pays the tax does not depend on who writes the check to the government.

    b. the consumer pays all of the tax.

    c. the government gets revenue, and the tax creates additional producer surplus.

    d. All of the answers are correct.

14. With a commodity tax,

    a. who pays the tax depends on who writes the check to the government.

    b. who pays the tax does not depend on the relative elasticities of supply and demand.

    c. the government gets revenue, and the tax creates a wedge between the price buyers pay and the price sellers get.

    d. All of the answers are correct.

15. With a commodity subsidy,

    a. who benefits does not depend on who gets the check from the government.

    b. who gets the subsidy depends on the relative elasticities of supply and demand.

    c. there are deadweight losses.

    d. All of the answers are correct.

Answers to Self-Practice Questions

1. d, Topic: Commodity Taxes
2. c, Topic: Commodity Taxes
3. a, Topic: Commodity Taxes
4. a, Topic: Commodity Taxes
5. c, Topic: Commodity Taxes
6. b, Topic: Commodity Taxes
7. b, Topic: Commodity Taxes
8. c, Topic: Commodity Taxes
9. b, Topic: Commodity Taxes
10. c, Topic: Commodity Taxes
11. c, Topic: Subsidies
12. c, Topic: Subsidies
13. a, Topic: Commodity Taxes
14. c, Topic: Commodity Taxes
15. d, Topic: Subsidies

7

The Price System: Signals, Speculation, and Prediction

Learning Objectives

In this chapter you will learn about the functions that markets serve. The topics covered are:

> Markets Link the World
> Markets Link to Each Other
> Solving the Great Economic Problem
> A Price Is a Signal Wrapped Up in an Incentive
> Speculation
> Signal Watching
> Prediction Markets

Summary

Much cooperation takes place in the world through markets. The baker does not bake a loaf of bread because he knows you want bread. He bakes bread because he decides that baking a loaf of bread is the best use of his resources. By reacting to market signals and acting in his own self-interest, the baker also serves others.

The market connects everything. Your choice to buy a product says that it is worth more to you than any other product that you could buy for the same or lower price. In other words, it is worth more to you than any other product from any place in the world. The market thus connects people around the world.

The market is like a computer because it processes huge amounts of information. It solves the **great economic problem** of how to allocate limited resources to best satisfy people's unlimited wants. The market works by using information and incentives.

The market, however, unlike many computers, does not have a central processing unit (CPU). Market decisions are decentralized, and any attempts to centrally plan markets fail due to lack of information and lack of incentives on the part of the planner.

A market price is an incentive, a signal, and a prediction. It signals whether people want more or less of a good, and it gives people incentives to buy or sell the good based on a comparison of market price to the value they place on the item. It also gives firms an incentive to produce more or less of a good. Market price is a prediction of the value of a good. If the expected future value rises or falls, current market prices will also rise or fall.

Speculation is the attempt to profit from future changes in prices. Its function in the market is to smooth out price fluctuations. If the price of a product is expected to rise in the future, speculators will push the price up today by buying the item expected to be more valuable in the future. What this really means is that the price changes less than it would have without speculation. Speculators often buy and hold for future sales. As a result, speculation often allows for more of the product to be available in the future when it is expected to be relatively scarce. Similarly, if the price of a good is expected to fall in the future, speculators will push the price down today by selling the item expected to be less valuable in the future. By their actions, speculators can cause the future price not to rise or fall as much as it would have in the absence of speculation.

A **futures** contract is a standardized contract to buy or sell specific quantities of a commodity or financial instrument at a specified price with delivery set at a specified time in the future. A **prediction market** is a speculative market carefully designed so that prices can be interpreted as probabilities and then used to make predictions. Prediction markets can be used to overcome information problems in large organizations.

Key Terms

great economic problem how to arrange our limited resources to satisfy as many of our infinite wants as possible

speculation an attempt to profit from future price changes

futures standardized contracts to buy or sell specified quantities of a commodity or a financial instrument at a specified price, with delivery set at a specified time in the future

prediction market a speculative market designed so that prices can be interpreted as probabilities and used to make predictions

Traps, Hints, and Reminders

Speculation tends to smooth price fluctuations. When speculation is barred, we then expect more variance in prices over time.

The prices in predictions markets can be interpreted as the probabilities of an event happening.

Like a huge computer, the market processes a huge amount of information and solves very complex problems, but unlike a computer, it does not have a central processing unit (CPU)—the market is voluntary and undirected.

Homework Quiz

1. Free markets encourage
   a. cooperation.
   b. corruption.
   c. confrontation.
   d. All of the answers are correct.

2. The free market is
   a. centrally planned.
   b. lacking in incentives.
   c. undirected.
   d. All of the answers are correct.

3. The price of a good in a free market is
   a. unfair.
   b. fair.
   c. the value of the good in its next-highest-value use.
   d. determined by the number of hours the good takes to produce.

4. Free market prices are
   a. signals.
   b. predictions.
   c. incentives.
   d. All of the answers are correct.

5. By purchasing a particular product, buyers are saying
   a. they would rather spend that money on this good than any other.
   b. they have no choice in the matter.
   c. their money is not worth much.
   d. the value they put on the good is less than the price.

6. The free market connects people

   a. locally.

   b. nationally.

   c. around the world.

   d. The free market does not connect people.

7. Speculation

   a. is immoral.

   b. should always be illegal.

   c. is the attempt to profit from future price changes.

   d. All of the answers are correct.

8. If the price of oil is expected to fall in the future, speculators will

   a. buy more oil today, driving down its current price.

   b. buy less oil today, driving down its current price.

   c. buy less oil today, driving up its current price.

   d. buy more oil today, driving up its current price.

9. Without speculation

   a. consumers would be better off.

   b. prices would change more.

   c. the free market would work more efficiently.

   d. All of the answers are correct.

10. If the price of coffee is expected to rise in the future, speculation

   a. increases the amount that the price of coffee will rise in the future.

   b. has no effect on the increase in the price of coffee in the future.

   c. decreases the amount that the price of coffee will rise in the future.

   d. has an unpredictable effect on change in coffee prices in the future.

11. Futures are

   a. standardized contracts for the right to buy or sell at a set price and time in the future.

   b. markets in which prices are probabilities that can be used to predict.

   c. standardized contracts to buy or sell at a set price and time in the future.

   d. products that do not yet exist.

12. Prediction markets have

   a. prices that can be interpreted as costs.

   b. outputs that can be interpreted as probabilities.

   c. prices that can be interpreted as probabilities.

   d. outputs that can be interpreted as costs.

13. A problem with centrally planning an economy is that the central planners lack

 a. resources.

 b. all the information the market has.

 c. government power.

 d. All of the answers are correct.

14. Central planning failed because central planners

 a. lack incentives to do what the public wants.

 b. had little control.

 c. had too much information.

 d. had too few resources.

15. The rose-growing worker in Kenya must know

 a. what the customer will do with the rose.

 b. why the customer wants the rose that time of year.

 c. nothing about the customer.

 d. everything about the customer.

Self-Practice Questions

1. The free market is

 a. centrally planned.

 b. voluntary.

 c. coercive.

 d. All of the answers are correct.

2. The price of a good in a free market is

 a. too high.

 b. too low.

 c. the value of the good in its next-highest-value use.

 d. determined by the government.

3. Free market prices are

 a. signals.

 b. set by the government.

 c. unfair.

 d. useless.

4. By purchasing a particular product, buyers are saying

 a. the product is the highest-value use of that amount of their money.

 b. they have too little money to buy something else.

 c. the value they put on the good is less than the market price.

 d. All of the answers are correct.

5. The free market connects people
   a. by force.
   b. who know each other.
   c. around the world. ✓
   d. The free market does not connect people.

6. Speculation
   a. reduces price fluctuations.
   b. moves some of the good from the time it is abundant to the time in the future that it is expected to be scarce.
   c. is attempting to profit from future price changes.
   d. All of the answers are correct. ✓

7. If the price of gold is expected to fall in the future, speculators will
   a. sell more gold today, driving down its current price. or buy less today ✓
   b. sell less gold today, driving down its current price.
   c. sell more gold today, driving up its current price.
   d. sell less gold today, driving up its current price.

8. Speculators
   a. help the market send the correct signal.
   b. reduce price fluctuations.
   c. moderate future price changes.
   d. All of the answers are correct. ✓

9. If the price of coffee is expected to rise in the future, speculation
   a. increases the amount that the price of coffee will rise in the future.
   b. has no effect on the increase in the price of coffee in the future.
   c. decreases the amount that the price of coffee will rise in the future. ✓
   d. has an unpredictable effect on the change in coffee prices in the future.

10. Futures
   a. are immoral.
   b. are moderate price changes in a market. ✓
   c. enable the current market to have more price instability.
   d. are products that do not yet exist.

11. Prediction markets
   a. serve no economic function.
   b. can be used to give decision makers in big organizations information that only subordinates have. ✓
   c. are always correct in their predictions.
   d. are only useful for betting on outcomes.

12. A problem with centrally planning an economy is that the central planners lack

  a. the ability to alter market outcomes.

  b. the ability to process all the information the market can process.

  c. government power to set prices.

  d. All of the answers are correct.

13. Central planning fails because central planners have

  a. different goals than the public.

  b. little power to affect the public.

  c. more information than they can process.

  d. too few resources to plan.

14. The rose-growing worker in Kenya must know

  a. how many others are producing roses.

  b. they get paid more for roses delivered around February 14.

  c. the price of other flowers.

  d. everything about the rose market.

15. The free market is

  a. voluntary.

  b. undirected.

  c. incentive driven.

  d. All of the answers are correct.

Answers to Self-Practice Questions

1. b, Topic: Markets Link the World

2. c, Topic: Markets Link the World

3. a, Topic: Markets Link the World

4. a, Topic: Markets Link the World

5. c, Topic: Markets Link the World

6. d, Topic: Speculation

7. a, Topic: Speculation

8. d, Topic: Speculation

9. c, Topic: Speculation

10. b, Topic: Speculation

11. b, Topic: Prediction Markets

12. b, Topic: Solving the Great Economic Problem

13. c, Topic: Solving the Great Economic Problem

14. b, Topic: Markets Link the World

15. d, Topic: Markets Link the World

8

Price Ceilings and Floors

Learning Objectives

This chapter discusses price ceilings and price floors and the effects of each on a market. The topics covered are:

> Price Ceilings
> Rent Control
> Arguments for Price Controls
> Universal Price Controls
> Price Floors

Summary

A **price ceiling** is a maximum price allowed by law. Most interesting are effective or binding price ceilings. To be effective, a price ceiling must be below the equilibrium price. If Congress passed a law stating that soft drinks could not sell for more than $100 each, such a price ceiling would not bind the market and, as such, it would have no effects in the current economy. Binding price ceilings create five important effects—shortages, reductions in product quality, wasteful waiting in line and other search costs, a loss of gains from trade, and a misallocation of resources.

That price ceilings cause shortages can be seen in Figure 8.1, where P_e and Q_e are the equilibrium price and quantity.

With the price ceiling below P_e, people want to buy Q_d of the good but producers want to sell Q_s of the good. Thus, there is a shortage of $Q_d - Q_s$ in the market.

Figure 8.1

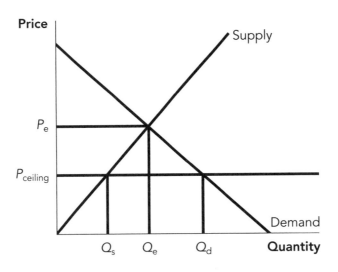

$Q_s < Q_d$.

① give **ss** less

② reduce Q & cost

Sellers have more customers than goods they want to sell at the ceiling price. One way they can react is to give the customer less. Another way to do this is to reduce quality. Making their product cheaper is a way the producer can bring their costs more in line with the price ceiling. For example, reductions in quality can be less meat in a price-controlled sandwich. A reduction in service, such as having customers get their own drink is another way to lower quality and costs.

Since, with a price ceiling, there are more people who want to buy goods than there are goods being offered for sale, price is not allocating the good. Somehow the good must still be allocated. If no other allocation scheme is used, then a "first-come, first-served" scheme will be used. Since not everyone who wants to consume at the ceiling price will get the good, some customers will start arriving early to make sure that they get the good. Thus, we have people spending a valuable resource, that is, their time, to consume the product, yet the seller does not receive the value of that time. So that resource is wasted. In addition, since there is a shortage, customers will not be sure who has the product in stock. Thus, consumers will waste more resources in search of the product. The limit on these search costs is the point at which the price ceiling plus the search cost equals a consumer's willingness to pay.

There are also lost gains from trade, or deadweight losses, with a price ceiling. This can be seen in Figure 8.2, where the equilibrium price is $10 and the price ceiling is $5.

With the $5 price ceiling, quantity demanded is 100 units and quantity supplied is 50 units, so the shortage, $Q_d - Q_s$, is 50. There are 50 units sold. So for every unit between 50 and the market equilibrium of 75, there are unexploited gains from trade. Put another way, for each unit between 50 and 75, consumers are willing to pay more than it would take to get producers to supply that unit. Thus, area $A + B$ is the lost gains from trade, or **deadweight loss,** associated with the price ceiling of $5.

Finally, a price ceiling creates a misallocation of resources. With the price system, those who are willing to pay the market price get the item and those who are not willing to pay the market price forego the good. With the price ceiling, the buyer who

Figure 8.2

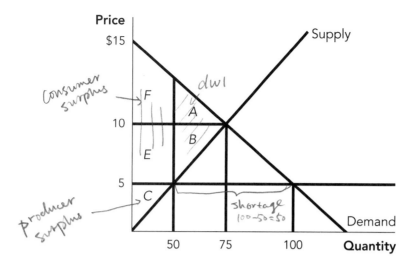

is willing to pay the most may or may not get to consume the good. A price ceiling therefore encourages bribery, for example, by selling to friends first or by bypassing the means to purchase the good (e.g., selling to someone "offline", when the only legal way the good can be purchased involves waiting in line).

If somehow, the consumers with the highest willingness to pay were able to get the good in Figure 8.2, then consumer surplus would be area $F + E$ and producer surplus would be area C. But if people arrive randomly, then the average value of (\$5 + \$15)/2, or \$10, is the appropriate comparison and consumers only gain E rather than $F + E$. The loss of F is due to the misallocation of the good. An example of this would be people in a warm state heating their pool with price-controlled fuel, while people in a cold state not being able to buy enough fuel to heat their house.

Rent control is a regulation that prevents rents from rising to equilibrium levels. As with any other price ceiling, rent control creates a shortage. Rent control also leads to landlords not keeping up with the maintenance on their properties. Rent control leads as well to people wasting valuable resources searching for available properties. There are deadweight losses or lost gains from trade with rent control. Why? Because some people, those who are looking to rent, are willing to pay more than some landlords charge, yet, with rent control, these potential renters are not able to rent. Finally, with rent control, resources are misallocated, since fewer apartments are constructed and people often end up living in an apartment that is smaller or bigger than their optimal choice.

Rent controls and other price ceilings often start with a "freezing" of prices or rents due to public pressure against prices or rents rising too quickly. As we learned in Chapter 4, supply in a shorter time frame is relatively inelastic. So, at first there is not a huge impact on quantity supplied, and the shortage is therefore not huge. But over time, the shortage grows since the supply is more elastic over a longer time frame. Politicians who pass rent control or other price ceiling laws operate over short election cycles (from 2 to 6 years). So if they see "freezing" rents as a way to get reelected, then politicians may think that a price ceiling is worth implementing, even if the public does not support price ceilings or rent controls. A **price floor** is a minimum price allowed by law. The most interesting ones are effective or binding price floors. To be effective, a price floor must be above the equilibrium price. Binding price floors have four important effects—surpluses, a loss of gains from trade, wasteful increases in quality, and a misallocation of resources.

The effects of a price floor can be seen in Figure 8.3, where P_e and Q_e are the equilibrium price and quantity.

Figure 8.3

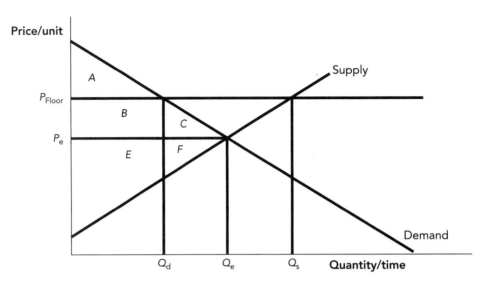

$Q_d < Q_s$
① give more
② raise Q

With the price floor above P_e, producers want to sell Q_s of the good, but consumers only want to buy Q_d. There is then a surplus of $Q_s > Q_d$ in the market.

Sellers have more of the good they want to sell at the price floor and not enough customers. Each firm is competing to attract customers, and a way they can attract them by giving them more. One way to do this is to raise quality. This is a waste in resources, however, since this higher quality is only used to attract customers who would be willing to buy at the current price and quality. The lost gains from trade, or deadweight losses, are area $C + F$. Finally, a price floor creates a misallocation of resources. With the price system, those who are willing to accept the market price get to sell the item, and those who are not willing to accept the market price forego selling the item. With the price ceiling, the sellers who are willing to sell at the lowest price may or may not get to sell the item.

Key Terms

price ceiling a maximum price allowed by law

deadweight loss the total of lost consumer and producer surplus when not all mutually profitable gains from trade are exploited. Price ceilings create a deadweight loss

rent control a price ceiling on rental housing

price floor a minimum price allowed by law

Traps, Hints, and Reminders

To be effective, a price ceiling must be below the equilibrium price.
To be effective, a price floor must be above the equilibrium price.
Rent control is a price ceiling on a particular type of good, such as rental housing units.
A deadweight loss is the same thing as a lost gain from trade.

Homework Quiz

1. A price floor is

   a. the maximum a consumer is willing to pay for a good.

   b. a maximum price allowed by law.

   c. the minimum a consumer is willing to pay for a good.

   d. a minimum price allowed by law.

2. A price floor causes

   a. surpluses.

   b. deadweight loss or lost gains from trade.

   c. misallocation of resources.

   d. All of the answers are correct.

3. An example of a price floor is

   a. gasoline price controls.

   b. the minimum wage.

   c. rent control. *price ceiling.*

   d. All of the answers are correct.

Figure 8.4

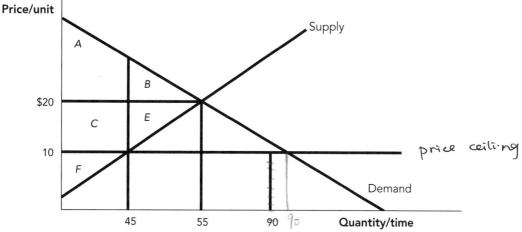

4. In Figure 8.4, a binding price ceiling would be

   a. $10.

   b. $20.

   c. $30.

   d. None of the answers is correct.

5. In Figure 8.4, the price ceiling quantity demanded is

   a. 40 units.

   b. 55 units.

   c. 90 units.

   d. None of the answers is correct.

6. In Figure 8.4, the price ceiling causes a shortage of
   a. 15 units.
   b. 35 units.   *90 − 45 = 45.*
   c. 50 units.
   d. None of the answers is correct.

7. In Figure 8.4, if those with the highest value of the good get to consume, then the deadweight loss associated with the price ceiling is area
   a. $A + B$.
   b. $B + E$.
   c. F.
   d. $A + C$.

8. In Figure 8.4, the price ceiling producer surplus is area
   a. $A + B$.
   b. $B + E$.
   c. F.
   d. $A + C$.

9. In Figure 8.4, if those with the highest value of the good get to consume, then consumer surplus with the price ceiling is area
   a. $A + B$.
   b. C.
   c. F.
   d. $A + C$.

10. In Figure 8.4, if the product is randomly allocated so that it is consumed by consumers with an average value for the product, then consumer surplus is area
   a. $A + B$.
   b. C.
   c. F.
   d. $A + C$.

11. In Figure 8.4, if the product is randomly allocated, the most resources that consumers would waste standing in line and/or searching for the good is area
   a. A.
   b. $B + E$.
   c. C.
   d. F.

12. In Figure 8.4, the extra loss in surplus due to random allocation compared to allocation to those with the highest value for the good, is area

    a. *A*.

    b. *B + E*.

    c. *C*.

    d. *F*.

13. Rent controls

    a. cause shortages.

    b. create lost gains from trade.

    c. misallocate resources.

    d. All of the answers are correct.

14. A minimum wage

    a. increases unemployment of low-wage workers.

    b. creates extra gains from trade.

    c. creates a shortage of workers.

    d. All of the answers are correct.

15. A price floor

    a. causes wasteful increases in quality.

    b. creates a shortage.

    c. increases gains from trade.

    d. leads to a better allocation of resources.

Self-Practice Questions

1. A price ceiling is

    a. the maximum a consumer is willing to pay for a good.

    b. a maximum price allowed by law.

    c. the maximum value of all the inputs used to produce the good.

    d. All of the answers are correct.

2. A price ceiling causes

    a. a shortage.

    b. a surplus.

    c. pressure on the producer to lower the price.

    d. pressure on consumers to offer lower prices.

3. An example of a price ceiling is

    a. farm price supports.

    b. the minimum wage.

    c. rent control.

    d. All of the answers are correct.

4. Price ceilings lead to

d

a. wasted resources.

b. consumers searching for product availability.

c. consumers waiting in line to buy the product.

d. All of the answers are correct.

5. With a price ceiling, if nothing else is set up, the good will be allocated by

a. income.

b. price.

c. a first-come, first-served scheme and by waiting in line.

d. All of the answers are correct.

Figure 8.5

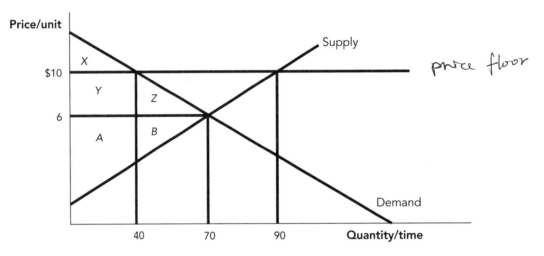

6. In Figure 8.5, a binding price floor would be

a. $0.

b. $6.

c. $10.

d. None of the answers is correct.

7. In Figure 8.5, with the price floor, quantity supplied is

a. 40 units.

b. 70 units.

c. 90 units.

d. None of the answers is correct.

8. In Figure 8.5, with the price floor, the amount of the surplus is

a. 20 units.

b. 50 units.   90 – 40

c. 90 units.

d. None of the answers is correct.

9. In Figure 8.5, with the price floor, consumer surplus is
   a. X.
   b. Z + B.
   c. A + B.
   d. Y.

10. In Figure 8.5, with the price floor, producer surplus is, at most
    a. X.
    b. Z + B.
    c. Y + A.
    d. Y.

11. In Figure 8.5, with the price floor, the deadweight losses from trade are at least area
    a. X.
    b. Z + B.
    c. A + B.
    d. Y.

12. The effects of rent controls are worse in the long run because
    a. the supply of rental units is more elastic in the long run.
    b. the supply of rental units is more inelastic in the long run.
    c. the demand for rental units is more elastic in the short run.
    d. the demand for rental units is unit-elastic in the long run.

13. With a price ceiling
    a. gains from trade are maximized.
    b. there are unexploited gains from trade.
    c. there are no trades made.
    d. the supply of goods is bought by the buyer with the highest willingness to pay.

14. With a price ceiling
    a. the quality of the good improves. ✗ $Q \downarrow$
    b. there is a surplus on the market. ✗   shortage
    c. resources are misallocated.
    d. All of the answers are correct.

15. With a price ceiling, goods may be allocated by all of the following EXCEPT
    a. bribery. 贿赂
    b. publicly announced price alone.
    c. personal connections.
    d. a first-come, first-served scheme and by waiting in line.

Answers to Self-Practice Questions

1. b, Topic: Price Ceilings

2. a, Topic: Price Ceilings

3. c, Topic: Price Ceilings

4. d, Topic: Price Ceilings

5. c, Topic: Price Ceilings

6. c, Topic: Price Floors

7. c, Topic: Price Floors

8. b, Topic: Price Floors

9. a, Topic: Price Floors

10. c, Topic: Price Floors

11. b, Topic: Price Floors

12. a, Topic: Rent Control

13. b, Topic: Price Ceilings

14. c, Topic: Price Ceilings

15. b, Topic: Price Ceilings

9

International Trade

Learning Objectives

In this chapter, we continue the study of exchange begun in Chapter 2. Topics covered are:

> Analyzing Trade with Supply and Demand

> The Costs of Protectionism

> Arguments against International Trade

Summary

The economics of trade does not vary, whether it is between two parties within a country, or two parties in different countries. Trade takes place when both sides expect to gain. There are, however, political issues associated with trade between two parties in different countries.

Gains from free trade can be seen graphically in Figure 9.1, where $5 and 100 units are the equilibrium price and quantity if there is no trade.

With no trade, consumer surplus is area A, producer surplus is area $B + F$, and total surplus is area $A + B + F$. Once this market is opened up for free trade, then consumers can buy at the world price of $1. Then, consumer surplus is $A + B + C + E$, producer surplus is F, and total surplus is $A + B + C + E + F$. Thus, total surplus has grown by area $C + E$ or there are gains from trade of $C + E$.

Conversely, we can see what happens if the government imposes some type of protection on this market. **Protectionism** is an economic policy of restraining trade

Figure 9.1

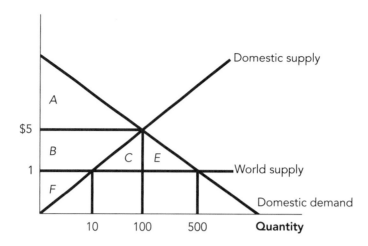

through quotas, tariffs, or other regulations that burden foreign producers but not domestic producers. A **trade quota** is a quantity restriction by which imports greater than the quota amount are forbidden. A **tariff** is a tax on imports.

In Figure 9.1, if the government imposed a quota or tariff large enough that none of the good was imported and price returned to the no-trade equilibrium, where domestic supply equals domestic demand, there will be lost gains from trade. As in the no-trade situation just discussed, consumer surplus is area *A*, producer surplus is area *B* + *F*, and total surplus is *A* + *B* + *F*. The gains from opening up the market to free trade, area *C* + *E*, are lost due to the protection. Area *E* is a consumption loss due to domestic consumers losing consumption they formerly had. Area *C* is an efficiency loss due to relatively inefficient domestic producers replacing relatively efficient foreign producers in supplying this good to the domestic market.

We can also model the effects of a tariff by using supply and demand analysis. Figure 9.2 shows what happens when a tariff is imposed on a free trade situation similar to that shown in Figure 9.1.

Figure 9.2

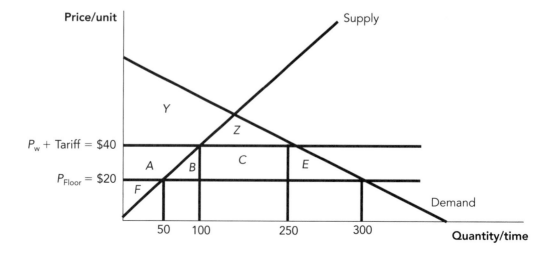

In Figure 9.2, with domestic free trade at the world price of $20, domestic production is 50 units and domestic consumption is 300 units. This means that imports are 250 units, with free trade. Consumer surplus is $Y + Z + A + B + C + E$, while producer surplus is F. Total surplus is $Y + Z + A + B + C + E + F$, with free trade.

Again in Figure 9.2, if a $20 per unit tariff is adopted, raising the domestic price from the world price of $20 to $40, then domestic production rises to 100 units, domestic consumption falls to 250 units, and imports fall to 150 units. Also due to the tariff, consumer surplus falls to $Y + Z$, while producer surplus rises to $C + H$. Government revenue is area C, the amount of imports, i.e., $250 - 100 = 150$, times the amount of the tariff of $20. Notice that the area of government revenue in Figure 9.2 equals $3,000. This means that total surplus after the tariff is area $Y + Z + A + C + F$. Notice that missing are areas $B + E$ from total surplus, with free trade. That makes $B + E$ the deadweight welfare loss due to the tariff.

With protection, the good is no longer sold by suppliers with the lowest costs. Since there are lost gains from trade with the protection, the sum of consumer plus producer surplus is no longer maximized.

Protectionism, in general, raises the price of an imported good by reducing supply in the domestic market. This leads to an increase in price of the domestic substitutes for the foreign good, also, since the supply of the good, domestic plus foreign, will be reduced.

Other issues are associated with international trade. One concern is the effect on wages. Wages depend on productivity and encouraging workers to move to relatively productive industries. International trade between two countries can cause wages in both countries to rise. With international trade, jobs are lost in some industries, but jobs grow in other industries. Keeping jobs via protectionism is very expensive; retraining displaced workers or somehow compensating workers who lost their jobs would be a better policy. Child labor is related to the income of the people of a country, as is free trade. So free trade, rather than restrictions on free trade, is the better policy to reduce child labor around the world. Some people argue for protection of certain strategic or national defense industries. Every industry will argue that it is strategic or important for national defense, and, if protected, will eventually become inefficient due to reduced competition.

Decreases in transportation costs, integration of world markets, and increased speed of communication have made the world seem smaller. This trend is sometimes called *globalization*. Some people think this is new or bad, but the world has only recently become as globalized as it was prior to World War I. To give up globalization is to give up the gains from international trade.

Key Terms

protectionism the economic policy of restraining trade through quotas, tariffs, or other regulations that burden foreign producers but not domestic producers

trade quota a restriction on the quantity of goods that can be imported—imports greater than the quota amount are forbidden or heavily taxed

tariff a tax on imports

Traps, Hints, and Reminders

Trade takes place, whether it occurs between individuals in a country or individuals in different countries, when both individuals expect to benefit.

A tariff is simply a tax; so it has many of the effects on a market that any other tax would.

Homework Quiz

1. Among the winners with a tariff on cars are
   a. domestic producers of cars.
   b. domestic consumers of cars.
   c. the economy as a whole.
   d. All of the answers are correct.

Figure 9.3

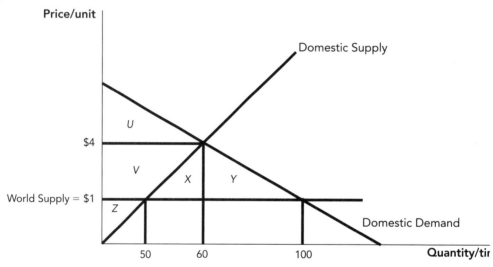

2. In Figure 9.3, with no international trade, consumer surplus is area
   a. *U.*
   b. *U + V + X + Z.*
   c. *V + Z.*
   d. *Z.*

3. In Figure 9.3, with no international trade, producer surplus is area
   a. *U.*
   b. *U + V + X + Y.*
   c. *V + Z.*
   d. *Z.*

4. In Figure 9.3, with no international trade, the total of producer and consumer surplus is
   a. U.
   b. $U + V + X + Y$.
   c. $V + Z$.
   d. Z.

5. In Figure 9.3, with international trade, imports are
   a. 20 units.
   b. 40 units.
   c. 80 units.
   d. 100 units.

6. In Figure 9.3, with international trade, consumer surplus is area
   a. U.
   b. $U + V + X + Y$.
   c. $X + Y$.
   d. Z.

7. In Figure 9.3, with international trade, producer surplus is area
   a. U.
   b. $U + V + X + Y$.
   c. $X + Y$.
   d. Z.

8. In Figure 9.3, with international trade, total surplus is
   a. U.
   b. $U + V + X + Y$.
   c. $X + Y$.
   d. Z.

9. In Figure 9.3, the gain from international trade is area
   a. U.
   b. $U + V + X + Y$.
   c. $X + Y$.
   d. Z.

10. In Figure 9.3, due to international trade, consumers
    a. gain V.
    b. lose V.
    c. gain $V + X + Y$.
    d. lose $V + X + Y$.

11. In Figure 9.3, due to international trade, producers

   a. gain *V*.

   b. lose *V*.

   c. gain *V* + *X* + *Y*.

   d. lose *V* + *X* + *Y*.

12. In Figure 9.3, if the market was protected to such an extent that all international trade stopped, then the deadweight loss would be

   a. $3.

   b. $60.

   c. $120.

   d. $240.

13. A tax on imports is called

   a. a comparative advantage.

   b. a tariff.

   c. an absolute advantage.

   d. a quota.

14. A restriction on the amount of imports to less than it would be with free trade is called

   a. a comparative advantage.

   b. a tariff.

   c. an absolute advantage.

   d. a trade quota.

15. According to the textbook, an argument made in favor of protection is that

   a. it increases total surplus

   b. it makes society better off.

   c. we need to protect some industries for national security reasons.

   d. All of the answers are correct.

Self-Practice Questions

1. Among the winners with a free trade on cars are

   a. domestic consumers of cars.

   b. the domestic government.

   c. the domestic economy as a whole.

   d. All of the answers are correct.

Figure 9.4

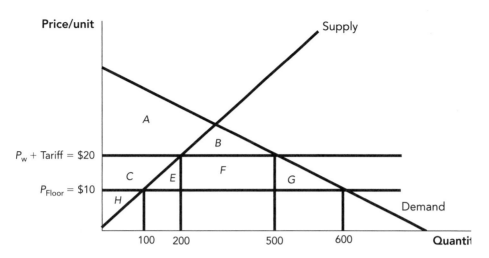

2. In Figure 9.4, with free international trade, consumer surplus is area

  a. $A + B$.

  b. $A + B + C + E + F + G$.

  c. $C + H$.

  d. H.

3. In Figure 9.4, with free international trade, producer surplus is area

  a. $A + B$.

  b. $A + B + C + E + F + G$.

  c. $C + H$.

  d. H.

4. In Figure 9.4, with free international trade, the total of producer and consumer surplus is area

  a. $A + B + C$.

  b. $A + B + C + E + F + G + H$.

  c. $A + C + H$.

  d. H.

5. In Figure 9.4, with free international trade, imports are

  a. 100 units.

  b. 300 units.

  c. 500 units.

  d. None of the answers are correct.

6. In Figure 9.4, with the tariff, consumer surplus is area

  a. $A + B$.

  b. $A + B + C + E + F + G$.

  c. $C + H$.

  d. H.

7. In Figure 9.4, with the tariff, producer surplus is area
   a. *A + B.*
   b. *A + B + C + E + F + G.*
   c. *C + H.*
   d. *H.*

8. In Figure 9.4, with the tariff, tariff revenue is area
   a. *A + B.*
   b. *F.*
   c. *E + G.*
   d. *H.*

9. In Figure 9.4, with the tariff, trade total surplus is
   a. *A + B.*
   b. *A + B + C + E + F + G.*
   c. *A + B + C + F + H.*
   d. *H.*

10. In Figure 9.4, the net loss from the tariff is area
   a. *A + B.*
   b. *F.*
   c. *E + G.*
   d. *H.*

11. In Figure 9.4, due to the tariff, trade consumers
   a. gain *C.*
   b. lose *C.*
   c. gain *C + E + F + G.*
   d. lose *C + E + F + G.*

12. In Figure 9.4, due to international trade, producers
   a. gain *C.*
   b. lose *C.*
   c. gain *C + E + F +G.*
   d. lose *C + E + F + G.*

13. In Figure 9.4, the government revenue from the tariff is
   a. $10.
   b. $1,000.
   c. $3,000.
   d. $5,000.

14. Free trade
   a. hurts the economy.
   b. increases total surplus.
   c. reduces imports.
   d. makes the people of a country worse off.

15. According to the textbook, an argument made in favor of protectionism is
   a. it increases total surplus
   b. it makes society better off.
   c. a country needs to protect its key industries.
   d. All of the answers are correct.

Answers to Self-Practice Questions

1. c, Topic: Analyzing Trade with Supply and Demand

2. b, Topic: Analyzing Trade with Supply and Demand

3. d, Topic: Analyzing Trade with Supply and Demand

4. b, Topic: Analyzing Trade with Supply and Demand

5. c, Topic: Analyzing Trade with Supply and Demand

6. a, Topic: The Costs of Protectionism

7. c, Topic: The Costs of Protectionism

8. b, Topic: The Costs of Protectionism

9. c, Topic: The Costs of Protectionism

10. c, Topic: The Costs of Protectionism

11. d, Topic: The Costs of Protectionism

12. a, Topic: The Costs of Protectionism

13. c, Topic: The Costs of Protectionism

14. b, Topic: Analyzing Trade with Supply and Demand

15. c, Topic: Arguments Against International Trade

10

Externalities: When Prices Send the Wrong Signals

Learning Objectives

In this chapter you will learn about the case when the market output is not the best. The topics you will learn about are:

> External Costs, External Benefits, and Efficiency
> Private Solutions to Externality Problems
> Government Solutions to Externality Problems

Summary

In the past several chapters we have seen that the free market maximizes total, the case when all costs are private costs. A **private cost** is a cost paid by the consumer or producer.

An **external cost** is a cost paid by people other than the consumer or producer trading in the market. **Social cost** is the cost to everyone: the private cost plus the external cost. When there are external costs, social costs are different than private costs. **Social surplus** is consumer surplus plus producer surplus plus everyone else's surplus. When there are external costs, social surplus is greater than the total of consumer surplus plus producer surplus.

These ideas are shown in Figure 10.1, where social costs are private costs or supply plus social costs.

Figure 10.1

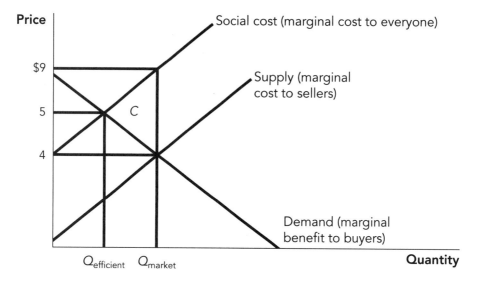

The **efficient quantity** is the quantity that maximizes social surplus. This quantity is determined by the point where social costs equal demand. The market quantity, where supply or private costs equal demand, is larger than the efficient quantity, showing that, if left alone, the market may produce too much of this good.

The deadweight loss associated with the market quantity is area C. In this area, private costs are less than demand, but social costs are greater than demand. Thus, for any unit produced past the efficient quantity, the costs to society are greater than any consumer's willingness to pay. In Figure 10.1, the last unit exchanged has a social cost of $9 but a benefit of only $4, so the deadweight loss is $5.

There can also be external benefits from a product. An **external benefit** is a benefit received by people other than the consumers and producers trading in the market. When there are external benefits, social benefits are greater than private benefits, and social surplus is greater than the total of consumer surplus plus producer surplus.

The case of an external benefit is shown in Figure 10.2, where this time the efficient quantity is greater than the market quantity. This is because the individuals who buy the

Figure 10.2

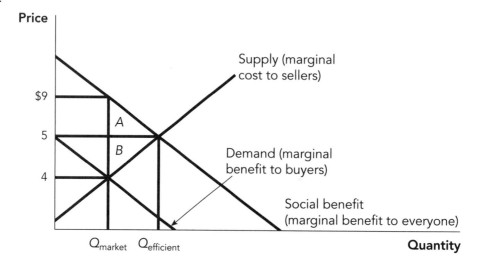

CHAPTER 10 • Externalities: When Prices Send the Wrong Signals • 101

product do not receive the external benefit and thus undervalue the product from society's point of view. For example, the next unit past the market quantity will cost a bit more than $4 to produce, say $4.01. Consumers of the good value it at less than $4, so it may not be produced even though society values it at a bit under $9, say $8.99. This is true of every unit up to the efficient output, the point at which social benefits equal supply. Thus the areas *A* + *B* are deadweight losses if only the market quantity is produced.

There are a number of potential solutions to the problems of external costs and benefits in a market. There are conditions under which private solutions are likely. There are also possible government solutions.

The **Coase theorem** shows that if transaction costs are low and property rights are well-defined, private bargains will ensure that the market solution is efficient even when there are externalities. **Transaction costs** are all the costs necessary to reach an agreement. Thus, under these conditions, the market will produce the efficient output and maximize social surplus even if there is an externality. For example, if the right to clean air is well-defined and transaction costs are low, breathers and polluters will bargain and agree to the socially optimal amount of air pollution.

Of course, at times the conditions required by the Coase theorem—well-defined property rights and low transaction costs—will not exist. In such cases, a government solution may improve on the market result. The simplest government solution is an optimal tax or subsidy. An optimal tax in the case of an external cost can lead to private costs equaling social costs, in which case the market will produce the efficient quantity and maximize social surplus. Similarly, in the case of an external benefit, an optimal subsidy can make consumers realize the social benefits and so lead to the market producing the efficient quantity and maximizing social surplus.

Another government solution is command and control, which occurs when the government tells the market how much to produce. The command and control solution is not very likely to produce efficient quantity and maximize social surplus. Tradable allowances are a type of command and control policy that may be more efficient. In such a policy the government sets limits, say, on pollution, but allows the producers to trade any amount as long as they are below their limit. By allowing this trade, the command and solution control is reached in the lowest-cost manner, since those firms whose reductions in pollution are expensive will buy allocations from firms that can reduce emissions more cheaply.

Key Terms

private cost a cost paid by the consumer or the producer

external cost a cost paid by people other than the consumer or the producer trading in the market

social cost the cost to everyone: the private cost plus the external cost

social surplus consumer surplus plus producer surplus plus everyone else's surplus

efficient equilibrium the price and quantity that maximizes social surplus

efficient quantity the quantity that maximizes social surplus

the Pigouvian tax a tax on a good with external costs

external benefit a benefit received by people other than the consumers or producers trading in the market

externalities external costs or external benefits that fall on bystanders

the Pigouvian subsidy a subsidy on a good with external benefits

the Coase theorem posits that if transaction costs are low and property rights are clearly defined, private bargains will ensure that the market equilibrium is efficient even when there are externalities

transaction costs all the costs necessary to reach an agreement

Traps, Hints, and Reminders

Costs should be counted regardless of who bears them.
Benefits should be counted regardless of who receives them.
Remember from Chapter 6 that it does not matter if it is a tax or a subsidy that is modeled as impacting supply or demand—you will get the same result in either case.
A problem in a market does not always call for a government solution. The Coase theorem shows that solutions are possible.

Homework Quiz

1. Social surplus includes
   a. consumer surplus.
   b. producer surplus.
   c. everyone else's surplus.
   d. All of the answers are correct.

2. A private benefit is received by
   a. consumers or producers.
   b. everyone other than consumers and producers of the good.
   c. some private persons not engaged in the trade.
   d. the government.

3. The market output with an external cost occurs when
   a. social costs equal demand.
   b. supply equals demand.
   c. social costs equal the marginal benefit to buyers.
   d. All of the answers are correct.

Figure 10.3

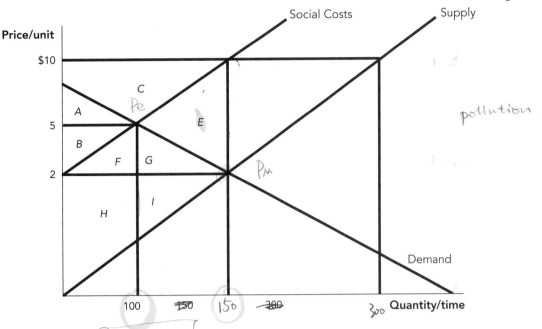

4. In Figure 10.3, the market output is
   a. 100 units.
   b. 150 units.
   c. 300 units.
   d. None of the answers is correct.

5. In Figure 10.3, the efficient output is
   a. 100 units.
   b. 150 units.
   c. 300 units.
   d. None of the answers is correct.

6. In Figure 10.3, the deadweight loss associated with the market output is area
   a. *A*.
   b. *F* + *G*.
   c. *E*.
   d. *H*.

7. In Figure 10.3, the area of the deadweight loss measures
   a. $50.
   b. $200.
   c. $400.
   d. None of the answers is correct.

$$\frac{10-2}{2} \times 50 = 200$$

8. In Figure 10.3, the value of wasted resources on the last unit produced in the market output is

   a. $2.

   b. $8.

   c. $10.

   d. None of the answers is correct.

9. In Figure 10.3, a way to get the market to the efficient solution would be

   a. an optimal tax.

   b. an optimal subsidy.

   c. the government taking over ownership of the market.

   d. All of the answers are correct.

10. Figure 10.3 shows the case of a(n)

   a. external cost.

   b. external benefit.

   c. price discriminator.

   d. price ceiling.

11. The government telling the people in a market how much to produce is called

   a. command and control.

   b. an optimal tax.

   c. an optimal subsidy.

   d. the Coase theorem.

12. Social benefit is

   a. private cost plus private benefit.

   b. private benefit plus external benefit.

   c. government cost plus social benefit.

   d. government cost plus external cost.

13. A private benefit is received by

   a. consumers or producers.

   b. everyone other than consumers and producers of the good.

   c. some private persons not engaged in the trade.

   d. the government.

14. The efficient output with an external benefit occurs when

   a. social costs equal demand.

   b. social surplus is maximized.

   c. supply equals demand.

   d. All of the answers are correct.

15. For there to be private solutions to externalities, there must be

    a. low transaction costs.

    b. untradable allowances.

    c. undefined property rights.

    d. All of the answers are correct.

Self-Practice Questions

1. Social cost is

    a. private cost plus private benefit.

    b. private cost plus external cost.

    c. government cost plus social benefit.

    d. government cost plus external cost.

2. A private cost is paid by

    a. consumers or producers.

    b. everyone other than consumers and producers of the good.

    c. some private persons not engaged in the trade.

    d. the government.

3. The efficient output with an external cost occurs when

    a. social costs equal demand.

    b. social surplus is minimized.

    c. social costs equal or are greater than the marginal benefit to buyers.

    d. All of the answers are correct.

4. Private surplus excludes

    a. consumer surplus.

    b. producer surplus.

    c. everyone else's surplus.

    d. All of the answers are correct.

5. A social cost is paid by

    a. consumers.

    b. the government.

    c. producers.

    d. everyone other than consumers and producers of the good.

6. The market output with an external cost occurs when

    a. social costs equal demand.

    b. supply equals demand.

    c. social costs equal the marginal benefit to buyers.

    d. All of the answers are correct.

7. A way that the government can encourage producers to lower pollution reduction cost is to

   a. use the Coase theorem.

   b. make the individual firms allowances tradable.

   c. ban trade in the allowances.

   d. have a government ceiling price on the allowances.

Figure 10.4

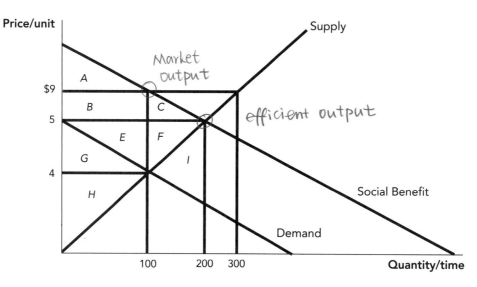

8. In Figure 10.4, the value of lost benefit on the last unit produced in the market output is

   a. $4.

   b. $5.

   c. $9.

   d. None of the answers is correct.

9. In Figure 10.4, a way to get the market to the efficient solution would be

   a. an optimal tax.

   b. an optimal subsidy. 最理想的补贴

   c. to have the government take over ownership of the market.

   d. All of the answers are correct.

10. Figure 10.4 shows the case of a(n)

   a. external cost.

   b. external benefit.

   c. price discriminator.

   d. price ceiling.

11. In Figure 10.4, the market output is

    a. 100 units.

    b. 200 units.

    c. 300 units.

    d. None of the answers is correct.

12. In Figure 10.4, the efficient output is

    a. 100 units.

    b. 200 units.

    c. 300 units.

    d. None of the answers is correct.

13. In Figure 10.4, the deadweight loss at the market output is area

    a. $A + B$.

    b. $E + F$.

    c. $C + F$.

    d. I.

14. In Figure 10.4, the deadweight loss measures

    a. $100.

    b. $250.

    c. $500.

    d. None of the answers is correct.

15. For there to be private solutions to externalities, there must be

    a. large transaction costs.

    b. tradable allowances.

    c. well-defined property rights.

    d. All of the answers are correct.

Answers to Self-Practice Questions

1. b, Topic: External Costs, External Benefits, and Efficiency

2. a, Topic: External Costs, External Benefits, and Efficiency

3. a, Topic: External Costs, External Benefits, and Efficiency

4. c, Topic: External Costs, External Benefits, and Efficiency

5. d, Topic: External Costs, External Benefits, and Efficiency

6. b, Topic: External Costs, External Benefits, and Efficiency

7. b, Topic: Government Solutions to Externality Problems

8. b, Topic: External Costs, External Benefits, and Efficiency

9. b, Topic: Government Solutions to Externality Problems

10. b, Topic: External Costs, External Benefits, and Efficiency

11. a, Topic: External Costs, External Benefits and Efficiency

12. b, Topic: External Costs, External Benefits, and Efficiency

13. c, Topic: External Costs, External Benefits, and Efficiency

14. b, Topic: External Costs, External Benefits, and Efficiency

15. c, Topic: Private Solutions to Externality Problems

11

Cost and Profit Maximization Under Competition

Learning Objectives

Learning about costs and profit maximization is fundamental to understanding the economics of a firm. The topics covered in this chapter are:

> What Price to Set?
> What Quantity to Produce?
> Profit and the Average Cost Curve
> Entry, Exit, and Shutdown Decisions
> Entry, Exit, and Industry Supply Curves

Summary

If the demand increases for a product, the industry producing it grows. If the demand decreases for a product, the industry producing it shrinks. The signal for this increase or decrease in production is profit. Profit is defined as:

$$\text{Profit} = \text{Total Revenue} - \text{Total Cost}$$

$$\text{or Profit} = TR - TC$$

where total revenue, TR, is price times quantity sold, and **total cost**, TC, is the cost of producing a given quantity of output.

To find the profit-maximizing output or quantity for a firm, it is convenient to look at the revenue from selling more than one more of the product compared to the cost of producing one more of the product. The revenue from selling one more unit of the product is called the firm's **marginal revenue,** *MC.* More formally, *MR* is the change in total revenue, *TR*, when output changes, or $\Delta TR/\Delta Q$. The cost of producing one more unit of the good is called the firm's **marginal cost,** *MC.* More formally, *MC* is the change in total cost, *TC*, when output changes, or $\Delta TC/\Delta Q$.

To maximize profit, a firm will produce any unit where marginal revenue, *MR,* is greater than marginal cost, *MC.* Any unit for which $MR > MC$ adds to profit. Any unit for which $MR < MC$ reduces profit. Thus, the profit-maximizing firm produces all units where $MR > MC$, and stops expanding output when $MR = MC$.

For a competitive firm, price, *P*, equals marginal revenue, *MR*. This is because a competitive firm can sell all it wants at the market price without changing the price.

Marginal cost, *MC*, for each firm in a competitive industry will equal the same price, *P*, and thus each firm in a competitive industry will have the same level or value of *MC*. That is not the same *MC* curve, but each firm will move along its *MC* curve until *MC* equals *P* so that the *MC* of each firm is the same value. This is the mechanism that minimizes the total cost of production in the industry. The logic is that if Firm 1 has an *MC* of $10 and Firm 2 has an *MC* of $6, then by having Firm 1 produce one less unit of the good (saving $10) and having Firm 2 produce one more of the good (at a cost of $6), the total cost of production is reduced by $10 − $6, or $4, but industry output does not change.

Fixed costs, *FC*, are those that do not vary with output. You should enter industries in which producer surplus less fixed cost is greater than zero. This is the same thing as saying that you should enter an industry when profit is greater than zero.

Average cost, *AC*, is total cost divided by output: $AC = TC/Q$. **Total revenue** is price times quantity, $P \times Q$. Since profit, as we define it, is total revenue minus total costs $(TR - TC)$ and firms enter industries with a profit greater than zero, then firms enter when $TR - TC > 0$ or when $TR > TC$. In addition, $TR > TC = P \times Q > TC$; thus, firms also enter if $P \times Q/Q > TC/Q$ or when $P > AC$.

Total cost, *TC*, the cost of producing a given quantity of output, can be broken down into fixed cost and variable cost. **Variable costs**, *VC*, are the costs that change with output. Variable cost is also the marginal cost for each unit produced that is added together, or the sum of the marginal cost of each unit produced. This means that the average cost can be expressed as follows:

$$AC = TC/Q = (VC/Q) + (FC/Q)$$

Also, profit can be calculated from average cost and price as follows:

$$\text{Profit} = (P - AC) \times Q$$

As fixed costs are spread over more and more units of production, average fixed costs decline and average cost, *AC,* also declines. For many industries, *AC* eventually becomes flat or begins to rise.

Some of the ideas discussed here are shown in Figure 11.1.

At P_1, the firm will produce Q_1, at which price (*P*) equals marginal cost (*MC*). However, notice that *AC* is greater than *P* at Q_1, so a competitive firm would lose money as $P < AC$ at that quantity. At P_2, the firm will produce Q_2. At this quantity, *AC* equals *P* and the firm is making a zero or normal profit. At P_3, the firm will produce Q_3 and makes a profit, as $P > AC$ at that quantity.

Figure 11.1

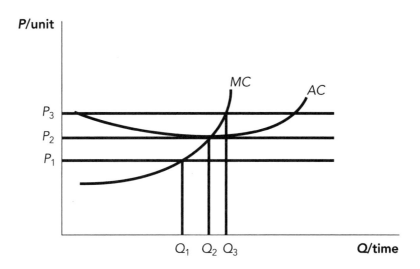

Sunk costs are costs that cannot be recovered, and thus they do not affect the decision of a firm to exit an industry. A firm will exit if $P - AC < 0$, or producer surplus less recoverable costs is less than zero. When there is uncertainty, the entry and exit decisions become related to lifetime profits rather than to profits today. Thus, a firm may not exit when price is below AC, if the firm expects price to rise in the future.

The industry supply curve is all the MC curves of all the firms in (or potentially in) the industry. As price rises, more firms will start producing, resulting in the industry supply curve becoming more elastic than the MC curves of individual firms.

The **long run** is the time it takes for substantial investment and entry to occur. The **short run** is when there cannot be entry.

In many industries, the AC is U-shaped in the long run (at first declining and then later rising). For other industries, the AC is flat or constant over a range of output. In the constant cost case, an increase in demand leads to a temporary increase in price and profits. The increase in profits induces other producers to enter into the business. Entrants are able to produce at the same AC of firms already in the industry, leading to a flat or constant AC. An industry in which AC is declining over the relevant range of output is a special case that is sometimes associated with a geographic clustering of firms in an industry.

Key Terms

long run the time it takes for substantial new investment and entry to occur

short run the time period before entry occurs

total revenue, TR, price times quantity sold: $TR = P \times Q$

total cost, TC, the cost of producing a given quantity of output

explicit cost a cost that requires a money outlay

implicit cost a cost that does not require a money outlay

economic profit total revenue minus total costs, including implicit costs

accounting profit total revenue minus explicit costs

fixed costs, *FC*, costs that do not vary with output

variable costs, *VC*, costs that do vary with output

marginal revenue, *MR*, the change in total revenue from selling an additional unit. For a firm in a competitive industry, $MR = P$

marginal cost, *MC*, the change in total cost from producing an additional unit

average cost, *AC*, the cost per unit, i.e., the total cost of producing Q units divided by Q: $AC = TC/Q$

zero profits or **normal profits** profits that occur when $P = AC$ and the firm is covering all of its costs, including enough to pay labor and capital and their ordinary opportunity cost

sunk costs costs that once incurred can never be recovered

increasing cost industry an industry in which industry costs increase with greater output; shown with an upward-sloped supply curve

constant cost industry an industry in which industry costs do not change with greater output; shown with a flat supply curve

decreasing cost industry an industry in which industry costs decrease with an increase in output; shown with a downward sloped supply curve

Traps, Hints, and Reminders

In the models used in this chapter, production equals sales. If $P > AC$, then the firm makes a profit.

When all firms set $P = MC$, industry's total costs are minimized for industry's output.

Since sunk costs cannot be recaptured, they do not affect the exit decision.

Entry will drive above-normal profits out of a competitive industry, and exit will drive below-normal profits (or losses) out of a competitive industry.

Homework Quiz

1. A competitive firm maximizes profit when

    a. total revenue equals total cost. $TR = TC$

    b. price equals average cost. $P = AC$

    c. price equals marginal cost. $P = MC$

    d. All of the answers are correct.

2. With competition, when price is greater than average cost,

    a. there will be entry in the industry in the long run.

    b. the firm is making an above-normal profit.

    c. the price will fall in the long run.

    d. All of the answers are correct.

Figure 11.2

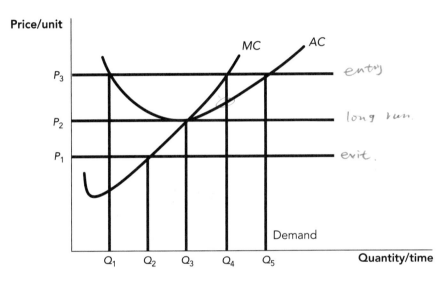

3. In Figure 11.2, at P_3, the firm will produce

    a. Q_1.

    b. Q_4.

    c. Q_5.

    d. None of the answers is correct.

4. In Figure 11.2, at P_1, the firm would be

    a. making a normal profit. P_1 : Produce Q_2

    b. making an above-normal profit.

    c. losing money.

    d. expecting entry into its industry.

5. In Figure 11.2, at P_3, the industry will see

a. the entry of new firms in the long run.

b. the exit of some firms in the long run.

c. each firm making a zero profit.

d. the price remaining the same over the long run.

6. In Figure 11.2, in the long run, we would expect the price to be

a. P_1.

b. P_2.

c. P_3.

d. None of the answers is correct.

7. Average cost is

a. $VC + FC.$ $=TC$

b. $AVC + FC/Q.$ $=ATC = \dfrac{TC}{Q}$

c. $MC + VC.$

d. All of the answers are correct.

8. If marginal cost is above average cost, then average cost is

a. at its minimum.

b. at its maximum.

c. falling.

d. rising.

9. Sunk costs 沉没成本，已支付成本

a. can be recaptured and do not affect a firm's exit decision.

b. cannot be recaptured and do not affect a firm's exit decision.

c. can be recaptured and do affect a firm's exit decision.

d. cannot be recaptured and do affect a firm's exit decision.

10. The short run is

a. less than a year.

b. when all factors of production are fixed.

c. the period before entry occurs.

d. All of the answers are correct.

all costs are variable in long run

边际收入　Δcost／ΔQ　TC－FC=VC　TC／Q

Table 11.1

Production or Sales	Marginal Revenue (P)	Marginal Cost	Variable Cost	Fixed Cost	Average Cost	Profit	
1	$6	$2	$2	$2　4	$4	$2	6×1 – 4
2	$6	$3	$5	$2　7	$3.5	$5	6×2 – 7
3	$6	$5	$10	$2　12	$4	$6	6×3 – 12

11. In Table 11.1, the fixed cost at three units of output is

　a. $2.

　b. $4.

　c. $5.

　d. $10.

VC +FC = TC

TC(下一个) = TC(上一个) + MC(下一个)

VC(下一个) = VC(上一个) + MC(下一个)

12. In Table 11.1, the variable cost at three units of output is

　a. $2.

　b. $4.

　c. $6.

　d. $10.

13. In Table 11.1, the average cost at three units of output is

　a. $4.

　b. $5.

　c. $6.

　d. $10.

AC= TC/Q.

14. In Table 11.1, the profit at three units of output is

　a. $4.

　b. $5.

　c. $6.

　d. $10.

profit = MR·Q – TC

15. Marginal cost

　a. rises when average cost falls.

　b. is cost divided by output.

　c. intersects average cost at average cost's minimum.

　d. All of the answers are correct.

└→相反

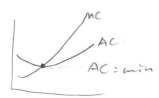

Self-Practice Questions

1. For a competitive firm, marginal revenue equals price because *[MR]*

   a. the firm's demand is downward sloping.

   b. the firm does not need to lower the price to sell more of its product. ✓ *MR=P=MC*

   max Profit

   c. marginal costs are falling. ✗

   d. average costs are increasing.

2. There will be entry in an industry when

   a. average costs are rising.

   b. sunk costs are positive.

   c. firms in the industry are making an above-normal profit.

   d. All of the answers are correct.

Figure 11.3

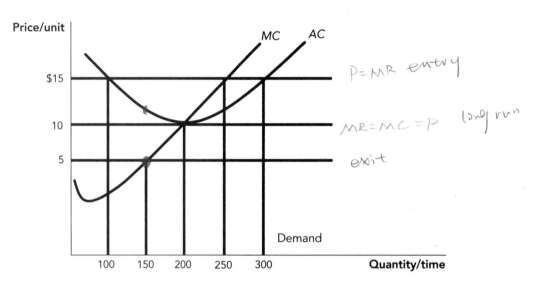

Handwritten notes: P=MR entry; MR=MC=P long run; exit

3. In Figure 11.3, at a price of $15, the firm will produce

   a. 100 units.

   b. 250 units. ✓

   c. 300 units.

   d. None of the answers is correct.

4. In Figure 11.3, at a price of $10 the firm would be

   a. making a normal profit. ✓

   b. making an above-normal profit.

   c. losing money. ✗

   d. expecting entry into its industry. ✗

5. In Figure 11.3, at $5, the industry will see

  a. an entry of new firms in the long run.

  b. an exit of some firms in the long run.

  c. each firm making a zero profit.

  d. the price remaining the same over the long run.

6. In Figure 11.3, in the long run, we would expect the price to be

  a. $5.

  b. $10.

  c. $15.

  d. None of the answers is correct.

7. Fixed costs are those that

  a. do not vary with output.

  b. do not change in the long run.

  c. are determined by the government.

  d. All of the answers are correct.

8. Average cost is

  a. TC/Q.

  b. $AVC + AFC$.

  c. $VC/Q + FC/Q$.

$$\frac{TC}{Q} = \frac{(VC + FC)}{Q} = \frac{VC}{Q} + \frac{FC}{Q}$$

  d. All of the answers are correct.

9. The long run is

  a. more than a year.

  b. when all factors of production are variable.

  c. the period before entry occurs.   Short run

  d. All of the answers are correct.

$$\frac{TC}{Q} \qquad MR \cdot Q - TC$$

Table 11.2

Output or Sales	Marginal Revenue	Marginal Cost	Variable Cost	Fixed Cost	Average Cost	Profit	
1	$5	$1	$1	$1 2	$2	$3	5×1 −2
2	$5	$2 1+2	$3	$1 4	$2	$6	5×2 −4
3	$5	$5 3+5	$8	$1 9	$3	$6	5×3 −9

10. In Table 11.2, fixed cost at three units of output is

  a. $1.

  b. $3.

  c. $4.

  d. $12.

11. In Table 11.2, variable cost at three units of output is

    a. $1.

    b. $3.

    c. $8.

    d. $12.

12. In Table 11.2, average cost at three units of output is

    a. $3.

    b. $4.

    c. $6.

    d. $12.

13. In Table 11.2, profit at three units of output is

    a. $4.

    b. $5.

    c. $6.

    d. $12.

14. Marginal cost

    a. falls when average cost falls.

    b. is the change in cost from producing one more unit of output.

    c. intersects average cost at an average cost's maximum.

    d. All of the answers are correct.

15. A decreasing-cost industry is one in which

    a. total cost falls as output rises.

    b. the supply curve is downward sloping.

    c. fixed cost falls as output rises.

    d. All of the answers are correct.

Answers to Self-Practice Questions

1. b, Topic: What Price to Set?

2. c, Topic: Entry, Exit, and Shutdown Decisions

3. b, Topic: What Quantity to Produce?

4. a, Topic: Profit and the Average Cost Curve

5. b, Topic: Entry, Exit, and Shutdown Decisions

6. b, Topic: Entry, Exit, and Shutdown Decisions

7. a, Topic: What Quantity to Produce?

8. d, Topic: What Quantity to Produce?

9. b, Topic: What Quantity to Produce?

10. a, Topic: What Quantity to Produce?

11. c, Topic: What Quantity to Produce?

12. a, Topic: What Quantity to Produce?

13. c, Topic: What Quantity to Produce?

14. b, Topic: What Quantity to Produce?

15. b, Topic: Entry, Exit, and Industry Supply Curves

12

No.

Competition and the Invisible Hand

Learning Objectives

This is a short but important chapter. The objective of this chapter is for you to learn about the optimality of competition. The topics covered include:

> Invisible Hand Property 1: The Minimization of Total Industry Costs
> Invisible Hand Property 2: The Balance of Industries
> Creative Destruction
> The Invisible Hand Works with Competitive Markets

Summary

This chapter focuses on the dynamics of competition—how competition works over time—and two invisible hand properties. **Invisible Hand Property 1:** even though no actor in a market economy intends to do so, in a free market, $P = MC_1 = MC_2 = \ldots MC_N$; as a result the total costs of production are minimized. **Invisible Hand Property 2:** entry and exit decisions not only work to eliminate profits, but they work to ensure that labor and capital move across industries to optimally balance production; thus the greatest use is made of limited resources.

The dynamics of competition illustrate the **elimination principle,** stating that above-normal profits are eliminated by entry into the industry, and that below-normal profits (or losses) are eliminated by exit from the industry. Joseph Schumpeter famously described the dynamics of competition as "creative destruction."

Key Terms

Invisible Hand Property 1 when an actor in a market economy does not intend to do so, yet in a free market $P = MC_1 = MC_2 = \ldots MC_N$; as a result the total costs of production are minimized

Invisible Hand Property 2 when entry and exit decisions not only work to eliminate profits, but also work to ensure that labor and capital move across industries to optimally balance production, thus making the greatest use of limited resources

elimination principle when above-normal profits are eliminated by entry, and below-normal profits are eliminated by exit

Traps, Hints, and Reminders

The economic cost curve includes a normal return or normal profit for the entrepreneur because normal profit is a cost of the firm being in business. The elimination principle thus still leaves competitive firms with a normal profit.

Entry will drive above-normal profits out of a competitive industry, and exit will drive below-normal profits (or losses) out of a competitive industry.

Homework Quiz

1. Competition through the invisible hand
   a. minimizes total cost.
   b. maximizes total revenue.
   c. maximizes total profits.
   d. minimizes total output.

2. Due to competition
   a. MC is greater than MR.
   b. MR is greater than MC.
   c. MC of all firms is the same.
   d. MR varies from firm to firm.

3. The competitive price in the long run will equal
   a. MC.
   b. AC.
   c. MR.
   d. All of the answers are correct.

4. In the long run, competitive firms will
   a. lose money.
   b. shut down.

    c. make a normal profit.

    d. make an above-normal profit.

5. The invisible hand assures that, with competition, limited resources are

    a. wasted.

    b. hoarded.

    c. destroyed by overuse.

    d. optimally balanced so they are put to the greatest use.

6. The elimination principle explains why in competition

    a. costs are maximized.

    b. above-normal profits do not persist.

    c. resources are wasted.

    d. All of the answers are correct.

7. The balance of industries property of competition is due to

    a. government regulation.

    b. barriers to entry.

    c. entry and exit.

    d. monopolies.

8. *Creative destruction* is a term used to describe

    a. monopoly.

    b. patents.

    c. the process of competition.

    d. government planning.

9. In competition, above-normal profits are a signal for

    a. entry or expansion of the industry.

    b. exit or contraction of the industry.

    c. the industry to shut down.

    d. government regulation of the industry.

10. Competition

    a. minimizes the total industry cost of production.

    b. optimally distributes labor and capital across industries.

    c. drives away above-normal profits.

    d. All of the answers are correct.

Self-Practice Questions

1. Competition minimizes total cost
   a. through government planning.
   b. even though no actor intends to do so.
   c. because customers require it.
   d. by law.

2. In competition, *MC* will equal
   a. the *MR* of the firm.
   b. the *MC* of all other firms in the industry.
   c. the price the firm faces.
   d. All of the answers are correct.

3. The greatest use is made of limited resources by means of
   a. entry and exit.
   b. barriers to entry.
   c. tariffs.
   d. All of the answers are correct.

4. Competitive firms will tend to make a normal profit in the long run due to
   a. the Peter principle.
   b. diminishing returns.
   c. the elimination principle.
   d. the theory of relativity.

5. The balance of industry property says that
   a. profits will be maximized.
   b. resources will be optimally distributed among industries.
   c. resources will be wasted by industries on balance.
   d. profits must be balanced against taxes.

6. The dynamics of competition have been described as
   a. planned destruction.
   b. planned obsolescence
   c. creative planning.
   d. creative destruction.

7. In the long run, with competition, profits will be
   a. negative.
   b. normal.
   c. above normal.
   d. unfair.

8. Above-normal profits are
   a. unearned revenue.
   b. theft from workers.
   c. a signal that taxes should be increased.
   d. a signal for entrepreneurs to move resources.

9. In competition, losses are a signal for
   a. entry or expansion of the industry.
   b. exit or contraction of the industry.
   c. the industry to shut down.
   d. government regulation of the industry.

10. Competition
   a. causes the MC of each firm in an industry to be the same.
   b. makes the greatest use of limited resources.
   c. leads to firms making a normal profit.
   d. All of the answers are correct.

Answers to Self-Practice Questions

1. b, Topic: Minimization of Total Industry Costs

2. d, Topic: Minimization of Total Industry Costs

3. a, Topic: The Balance of Industries

4. c, Topic: The Invisible Hand Works with the Competitive Market

5. b, Topic: The Balance of Industries

6. d, Topic: Creative Destruction

7. b, Topic: The Invisible Hand Works with the Competitive Market

8. d, Topic: The Invisible Hand Works with the Competitive Market

9. b, Topic: The Invisible Hand Works with the Competitive Market

10. d, Topic: The Invisible Hand Works with the Competitive Market

13

Monopoly

Learning Objectives

This chapter discusses a situation in which competition may not lead to a market producing the optimal quantity of a good. Both the problems and potential benefits of monopoly are covered. The topics in the chapter are:

> Market Power
> How a Firm Uses Market Power to Maximize Profit
> The Cost of Monopoly: Deadweight Losses
> The Costs of Monopoly: Corruption and Inefficiency
> The Benefits of Monopoly: Incentives for Research and Development
> Economies of Scale and the Regulation of Monopoly
> Other Sources of Market Power

Summary

This chapter covers the topic of **monopoly**. **Market power** is defined as the ability to raise price above average cost without fear that other firms will enter the industry.

The chapter shows how to find a monopoly's **marginal revenue (MR)**, the change in total revenue from selling an additional unit, given its demand curve. When the monopolist's demand is linear and downward sloping, its marginal revenue is linear, downward sloping and twice as steep as its demand. Marginal revenue for a change in output can be calculated from prices and quantities. For example, if at a price of $10, a firm sells 5 units, then its total revenue at 5 units is $50. If when the firm drops its price to $9, it sells 6 units, then the firm's total revenue at 6 units is $54. In this example, the marginal revenue from selling the 6th unit is $54 − $50 or $4.

The chapter further shows how to determine the *monopoly output* and *monopoly price.* As shown in Figure 13.1, the monopoly output, Q_m, is that quantity below the intersection of marginal revenue and **marginal costs (MC)**, that is, $MR = MC$.

Figure 13.1

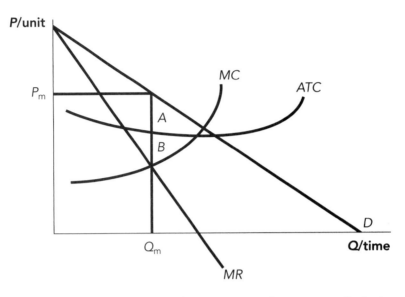

The monopoly price, P_m, is that price on the monopolist's demand curve above where $MR = MC$. Put another way, it is the price people are willing to pay for the monopoly quantity, Q_m.

One way to measure the cost of a monopoly is to measure the *deadweight loss* associated with that monopoly. The deadweight loss associated with a monopoly is the reduction in *total surplus*, that is, consumer plus producer surplus compared to the competitive outcome or where marginal costs equals demand or $MC = D$. In Figure 13.1, the deadweight loss is area A plus area B (or $A + B$).

Chapter 13 also shows how to find the *monopoly profit,* given the average total cost curve. The monopolist's profit is the difference between average revenue or price, P_m, and ATC at Q_m multiplied by the monopoly quantity, Q_m. In Figure 13.2, this is the rectangle bounded by points P_m, A, C, and B.

After the mechanics of monopoly have been covered, the issue of whether a particular monopoly is good or bad is taken up. Again, with a monopoly, one problem is that there is a deadweight loss or a reduction of total surplus below what it would be in a competitive market. However, with some types of monopolies the story is not so simple, and there can be trade-offs.

For example, *patent monopolies* for a new drug or medical device involve a trade-off between deadweight loss and innovation. Without the prospect of monopoly profits, the new drug or medical device may not be developed. In this type of situation, societies often choose to grant the monopoly, that is, the patent, and accept the deadweight loss to get the innovation.

Natural monopoly involves a trade-off between economies of scale and deadweight losses. Regulating of natural monopolies may offer a partial escape from this trade-off, but other issues, for example, product quality, may arise.

Figure 13.2

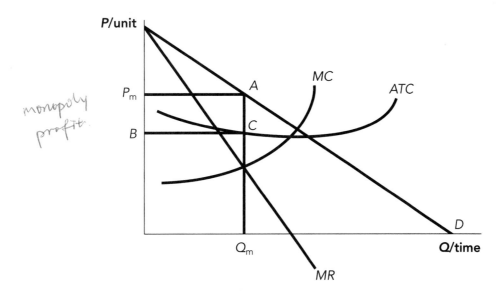

monopoly profit.

Many, maybe most, monopolies are neither patent nor natural monopolies; that is, they neither encourage innovation nor take advantage of economies of scale. They are usually created to transfer wealth to politically powerful elites. In such cases, the economic solution is to open the market to competition.

Key Terms

monopoly a firm with market power

market power the power to raise price above average cost without fear that other firms will enter the market

marginal revenue, MR, the change in total revenue from selling an additional unit

marginal cost, MC, the change in total cost from producing an additional unit. To maximize profit, a firm increases output until $MR = MC$

natural monopoly said to exist when a single firm can supply the entire market at a lower cost than two or more firms

economies of scale the advantages of large-scale production that reduce average costs as quantity increases

barriers to entry factors that increase the cost to new firms of entering an industry

Traps, Hints, and Reminders

Profit Maximization

A firm maximizes its profit by increasing output until marginal revenue, MR, equals marginal cost, MC. In competition price, P, equals MR while for monopoly, $MR < P$.

Marginal Revenue Shortcut

When demand is a downward-sloping straight line, marginal revenue, MR, is also a downward-sloping straight line, but it is twice as steep as demand.

Relationship of Monopoly Marginal Revenue to Demand

Monopoly marginal revenue is below demand because the monopoly perceives that, to sell more, it must lower the price on all units sold.

Calculating Total Revenue

Total revenue is price times quantity, so if at a price of $1 you sell 50 units, your total revenue is $50.

Calculating Marginal Revenue

Marginal revenue for a particular price change can be calculated by subtracting the total revenue from the first price, from the total revenue from the second price. For example, if at a price of $2 the total revenue is $100, and at a price of $1 the total revenue is $110, then the marginal revenue calculated by reducing the price from $2 to $1 is $110 − $100, which is $10.

Price $2   Price $1
TR $100   TR $110
MR = $110 − $100 = $10

Markup Over Cost

Remember that the more the demand is inelastic, the more the monopolist can mark up price above average total costs.

Homework Quiz

1. Market power is the ability to

a. raise price above average cost without fear that other firms will enter the industry.

b. raise average costs without fear that other firms will enter the industry.

c. influence government intervention in your industry.

d. raise marginal costs without fear that the other firms will enter the industry.

Figure 13.3

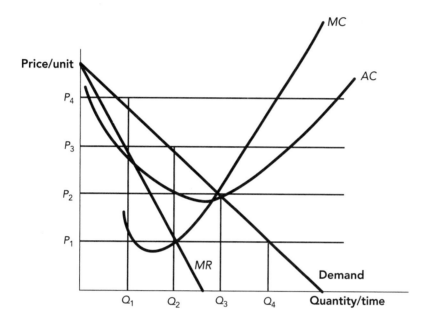

2. In Figure 13.3, the monopoly output is

a. Q_1.

b. Q_2.

c. Q_3.

d. Q_4.

3. In Figure 13.3, the monopolist will charge

a. P_1.

b. P_2.

c. P_3.

d. P_4.

4. In Figure 13.3, the firm is

a. losing money.

b. making a normal profit.

c. breaking even.

d. making an economic profit.

5. In Figure 13.3, an economist would want to

    a. allow entry and encourage competition.

    b. accept the deadweight loss to get economies of scale.

    c. regulate the industry.

    d. All of the answers are correct.

Figure 13.4

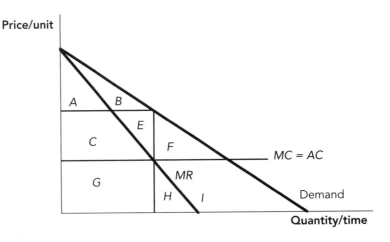

6. In Figure 13.4, the deadweight loss of monopoly is area

    a. $A + B$.

    b. $C + E$.

    c. F.

    d. $G + H + I$.

7. In Figure 13.4, the monopoly makes economic profits of area

    a. $A + B$.

    b. $C + E$.

    c. F.

    d. $G + H + I$.

8. A natural monopoly involves a trade-off between

    a. innovation and economies of scale.

    b. deadweight losses and economies of scale.

    c. deadweight losses and innovation.

    d. deadweight losses and market power.

9. A solution that economists offer for the monopoly problem is

    a. a government takeover of the market.

    b. a government ban on production of the good.

    c. opening the industry up to competition.

    d. having the government produce the good.

10. A drug can often be priced well above cost because of

a. market power.

b. the "you can't take it with you" effect.

c. the "other people's money" effect.

d. All of the answers are correct.

11. The deadweight loss associated with a monopoly is the

a. reduction in gains from trade due to deviations from competitive markets.

b. economic profits a monopoly makes.

c. total of producer and consumer surplus.

d. difference between monopoly price and marginal cost.

12. A monopolist recognizes that its marginal revenue (MR) is below demand because

a. its total cost increases with outputs.

b. it can charge whatever it wants for its product.

c. it must lower price on all units sold to sell more of its product.

d. it will make a profit at any output.

13. The economic reason for governments to grant patent monopolies is to

a. encourage innovation.

b. reward campaign donors.

c. capture economies of scale.

d. increase total surplus.

14. If a firm sells 100 units at a price of $20, and it sells 101 units at a price of $19, then its marginal revenue from selling the 101st unit is

a. $2,000.

b. $1,919.

c. $81.

d. −$81.

15. Economists view the deadweight loss associated with a monopoly as bad because it is captured by

a. the government.

b. consumers.

c. the monopolist.

d. no one.

Self-Practice Questions

1. An economic problem with a monopoly is that
   a. there is a loss in total surplus compared to the competition.
   b. monopolists produce too much of their product. $MC = MR$
   c. monopolists produce at the point where marginal cost equals marginal revenue.
   d. monopolists charge a price at the point where marginal revenue equals marginal cost. $MR = MC$

Figure 13.5

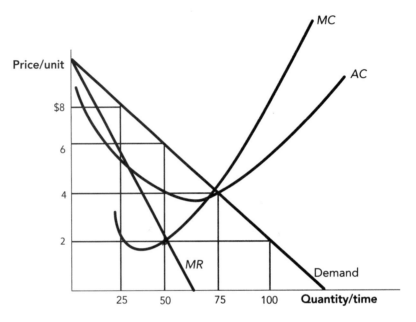

2. In Figure 13.5, the monopoly output is
   a. 25 units.
   b. 50 units. $MC = MR$
   c. 75 units.
   d. 100 units.

3. In Figure 13.5, the monopolist will charge
   a. $2. $8 - $2 = $6
   b. $4.
   c. $6.
   d. $8.

4. In Figure 13.5, the firm is
   a. losing money.
   b. making a normal profit.
   c. breaking even.
   d. making an economic profit.

5. In Figure 13.5, to get to the competitive solution, the government should

  a. allow entry and encourage competition.

  b. regulate the industry.

  c. grant the producer a patent.

  d. All of the answers are correct.

Figure 13.6

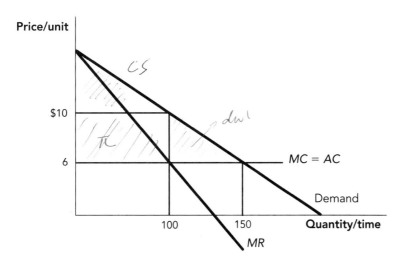

6. In Figure 13.6, the deadweight loss of monopoly is

  a. $4.

  b. $100.

  c. $200.

  d. $400.

$(10-6)(150-100) \times \frac{1}{2} = 4 \times 50 \times \frac{1}{2} = 100$

7. In Figure 13.6, the monopoly makes economic profits of area

  a. $4.

  b. $100.

  c. $200.

  d. $400.

$(10-6)100 = \$400$

8. A patent monopoly involves a trade-off between

  a. innovation and economies of scale.

  b. deadweight losses and economies of scale.

  c. deadweight losses and innovation.

  d. deadweight losses and market power.

9. The solution economists offer for the monopoly problem is

  a. a government takeover of the market.

  b. a government ban on production of the good.

  c. opening the industry up to competition.

  d. having the government produce the good.

10. A natural monopoly is characterized by

a. marginal costs rising with quantity.

b. average costs falling as quantity increases.

c. small fixed costs.

d. All of the answers are correct.

11. The ability of the monopolist to mark up price above costs is greater

a. when there is more inelastic demand.

b. when there is more elastic demand.

c. when demand is unitary elastic.

d. over a longer period.

12. The economic reason for governments to regulate decreasing cost monopolies is to

a. encourage innovation.

b. reward campaign donors.

c. capture economies of scale.

d. increase total surplus.

13. If a firm sells 100 units at a price of $11, and it sells 101 units at a price of $10, then the firm's marginal revenue from selling the 101st unit is

a. $1,100.

b. $1,010.

c. $90.

d. −$90.

$MR = 100 \times 11 - 101 \times 10$

$= 1100 - 1010$

$= 90$

$101 \times 10 - 100 \times 11 = -90$

14. Economists view the deadweight loss associated with a monopoly as bad because it is captured by

a. the government.

b. consumers.

c. the monopolist.

d. no one.

15. If a natural monopolist is forced to produce the competitive optimal quantity, it will

a. lose money.

b. make a normal profit.

c. break even.

d. make an economic profit.

Answers to Self-Practice Questions

1. a, Topic: The Cost of Monopoly: Deadweight Losses

2. b, Topic: How a Firm Uses Market Power to Maximize Profit

3. c, Topic: How a Firm Uses Market Power to Maximize Profit

4. d, Topic: How a Firm Uses Market Power to Maximize Profit

5. a, Topic: How a Firm Uses Market Power to Maximize Profit

6. b, Topic: The Cost of Monopoly: Deadweight Losses

7. d, Topic: How a Firm Uses Market Power to Maximize Profit

8. c, Topic: The Benefits of Monopoly: Incentives for Research and Development

9. c, Topic: The Cost of Monopoly: Deadweight Losses

10. b, Topic: Economies of Scale and the Regulation of Monopoly

11. a, Topic: Market Power

12. c, Topic: How a Firm Uses Market Power to Maximize Profit

13. d, Topic: How a Firm Uses Market Power to Maximize Profit

14. d, Topic: The Cost of Monopoly: Deadweight Losses

15. a, Topic: Economies of Scale and the Regulation of Monopoly

14

Price Discrimination

Bundling + Tying

Learning Objectives

This chapter covers price discrimination and why, surprisingly, it might not be such a bad thing. The topics covered are:

> Price Discrimination
> Price Discrimination Is Common
> Is Price Discrimination Bad?
> Tying and Bundling

Summary

Price discrimination is selling the same product at different prices to different customers. Here are just a few examples of price discrimination (this list is far from exhaustive):

> Student, military, and senior citizen discounts
> Time-of-day discounts, such as charging less for movie matinees or early dinners at restaurants
> Selling products in one country for more (or less) than you would sell them in other countries

If the demand curves are different, it is more profitable for a firm to set different prices in different markets than a single price that covers all markets. As seen in Figure 14.1, to maximize profit the monopolist should set a higher price in markets with

Figure 14.1

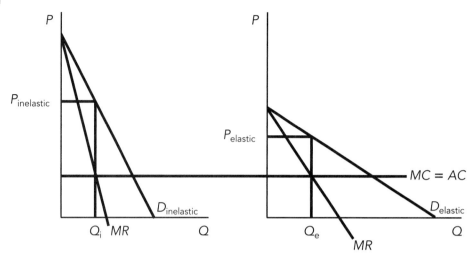

more inelastic demand, where Q_i is the quantity produced for demanders with the relatively inelastic demand and Q_e is the quantity produced for the demanders with the relatively elastic demand. As predicted, the demanders with the relatively inelastic demand are charged the higher price.

Arbitrage is taking advantage of price differences for the same good in different markets by buying low in one market and selling high in another market. Arbitrage makes it difficult for a firm to set different prices in different markets, reducing the profit from price discrimination. Thus, in order to price discriminate, a firm must be able to prevent arbitrage.

It is often easier to prevent arbitrage in services. If you go to a doctor or an attorney, you cannot generally sell the advice you received to someone else. With tangible goods, firms can sell differently marked goods to different segments of the market and then try to track the goods to determine if the lower-priced goods are being resold.

Perfect price discrimination is when each customer is charged his or her willingness to pay. This can be seen in Figure 14.2, where the perfect price discriminator charges the consumer who buys unit 1 exactly the maximum the consumer is willing to pay.

Then the perfect price discriminator charges the consumer who buys unit 2 at a slightly lower price, although it is still the most that the consumer is willing to pay. The perfect price discriminator keeps lowering the price, as it sells each additional unit until it sells unit $Q^\star$ to the last consumer at the maximum price that consumer is willing to pay, which is *MC*.

As can be seen in Figure 14.3, the perfect price discriminator captures all the gains from trade—that is, the shaded area.

Since the perfect price discriminators capture all the gains from trade, they have an incentive to maximize those gains, and unlike a single-price monopoly there are no deadweight losses. Put another way, the perfect price discriminator produces the point at which marginal costs equal demand, $Q^\star$ in Figure 14.3. This is exactly the quantity that would be produced if this market were competitive.

Since they produce the competitive output, perfect price discriminators create no deadweight losses. A less-than-perfect price discriminator may also increase total surplus compared to a monopolist with a single price. Price discrimination is most likely to increase total surplus when it increases output and when there are large fixed costs

Figure 14.2

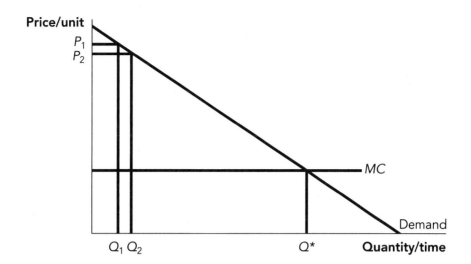

Figure 14.3

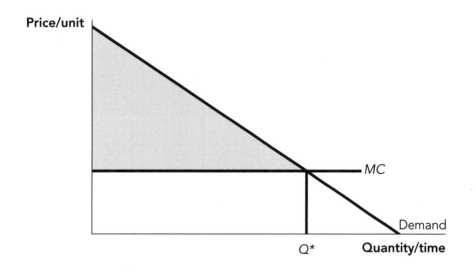

of development. By increasing output, price discrimination spreads fixed costs over more customers.

Tying is a form of price discrimination in which one good, called the base good, is tied to a second good, called the variable good. For example, printers are a base good and ink is a variable good. The variable good reveals the customer's intensity of use and thus his or her willingness to pay. A firm thus charges a low price for the base good and a high price for the variable good. Tying allows the firm to charge as many different prices as there are usage rates among customers.

Of course for tying to work as price discrimination, the firm must be able to prevent others from selling the variable good; that is, the base and variable goods must be actually tied in some manner. In the "printer-ink" example, sometimes the ink is tied to the printer by including a patented printer head on the ink cartridge.

Bundling is requiring that products be bought together in a bundle or package. A firm can sell some products either separately or together. For example, in Table 14.1, there are two customers and two channels.

The provider can either sell the channels separately to the two customers or the provider can bundle them. If the provider prices ESPN at $50 and AMC at $65, then

Table 14.1

	Maximum willingness to pay for ESPN	Maximum willingness to pay for AMC	Prices: ESPN=$50 AMC=$65 Revenue:	Bundle Price for ESPN and AMC = $70 Revenue:
Bill	$50	$20	$50 for ESPN	$70 for bundle
Mary	$10	$65	$65 for AMC	$70 for bundle
Company Revenues			$115	$140

only Bill buys ESPN and only Mary buys AMC, and company revenue is $115. However, if the provider bundles the channels and sells the bundle for $70, both will buy the bundle, as Bill values the two channels at $70 and Mary values them at $85. In this example, bundling will increase company revenue to $140. (Note that if the provider priced ESPN at $10 and AMC at $20 to maximize sales, both customers would buy both channels, but company revenue would be even lower, at $60.)

Bundling is a form of price discrimination because the company is basically charging Bill a low price for AMC and a high price for ESPN, while simultaneously charging Mary a low price for ESPN and a high price for AMC. As is often true in other cases of price discrimination, output is increased.

Key Terms

price discrimination selling the same product at different prices to different customers

arbitrage taking advantage of price differences for the same good in different markets by buying low in one market and then selling high in another market

perfect price discrimination (PPD) when each customer is charged his or her maximum willingness to pay

tying a form of price discrimination in which one good, called the base good, is tied to a second good, called the variable good

bundling requiring that products be bought together in a bundle or package

Traps, Hints, and Reminders

Remember that the price discriminator charges a higher price to the customers with a more inelastic demand.

Arbitrage, buying low in one market and selling at a higher price in another market, is usually legal. It was only illegal in the example in the book because Combivir was patent protected.

Tying does not mean the goods are always bought together. Generally, they are bought together at the initial purchase, but the variable good is often bought alone later.

Bundling does imply that the bundled goods are all purchased at the same time.

Perfect price discrimination (PPD) is perfect in the sense that each customer is charged exactly the maximum he or she is willing to pay for what is purchased.

Homework Quiz

1. Price discrimination

    a. always reduces gains from trade.

    b. may increase gains from trade.

    c. always maximizes gains from trade.

    d. does not affect gains from trade.

2. Arbitrage

    a. may make price discrimination impossible.

    b. takes advantage of price differences for the same good in different markets by buying low in one market and selling high in another market.

    c. reduces the profits from price discrimination.

    d. All of the answers are correct.

3. A price discriminator charges a

    a. lower price to customers with a more inelastic demand.

    b. single price to all customers.

    c. lower price to customers with a more elastic demand.

    d. higher price to customers with a more elastic demand.

4. To succeed at price discrimination, a firm must

    a. be competitive.

    b. prevent arbitrage.

    c. eliminate deadweight losses.

    d. prevent tying.

5. Perfect price discriminators

    a. maximize gains from trade.

    b. eliminate deadweight losses.

    c. increase output to the competitive quantity.

    d. All of the answers are correct.

Figure 14.4

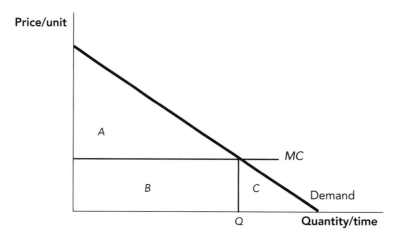

6. If the firm in Figure 14.4, is a perfect price discriminator, then the gains from trade will be
   a. area *A*.
   b. area *B*.
   c. area *C*.
   d. zero.

7. If the firm in Figure 14.4 is a perfect price discriminator, then the deadweight loss associated with perfect price discrimination will be
   a. area *A*.
   b. area *B*.
   c. area *C*.
   d. zero.

8. In economic terms, price discrimination is bad if
   a. output is increased.
   b. output stays the same or falls.
   c. there is arbitrage.
   d. the firm is able to prevent arbitrage.

9. With tying, the firm will sell _____ at a high price.
   a. a bundle of products
   b. the variable product
   c. the base product
   d. each individual product

10. When tying products, a firm must somehow be sure competitors cannot produce
    a. its base product.
    b. its bundle of products.
    c. its variable product.
    d. arbitrage.

Table 14.2

	Maximum willingness to pay for MTV	Maximum willingness to pay for FNC
Bill	$70	$20
Mary	$15	$80

11. In Table 14.2, if the provider prices MTV at $70 and FNC at $80, then the firm will have a revenue of
    a. $0.
    b. $70.
    c. $150.
    d. $185.

12. In Table 14.2, if the provider prices MTV at $70 and FNC at $80, then
    a. Mary will buy MTV but not FNC, and Bill will buy FNC but not MTV.
    b. both Mary and Bill will buy MTV and FNC.
    c. Mary will buy FNC but not MTV, and Bill will buy MTV but not FNC.
    d. neither Mary nor Bill will buy either channel.

13. In Table 14.2, if the provider bundles MTV and FNC at a price of $90, then the firm will have revenue of
    a. $0.
    b. $90.
    c. $150.
    d. $180.

14. In Table 14.2, if the provider bundles MTV and FNC at a price of $90, then
    a. Mary will buy the bundle but not Bill.
    b. Bill will buy the bundle but not Mary.
    c. Mary and Bill will both buy the bundle.
    d. neither Mary nor Bill will buy the bundle.

15. Bundling
    a. makes customers buy a low-quality product to get a high-quality one.
    b. reduces output and gains from trade.
    c. creates a deadweight loss.
    d. requires that products be bought together in a package or bundle.

Self-Practice Questions

1. Firms want to price discriminate because it
   a. increases profits.
   b. reduces deadweight losses.
   c. maximizes gains from trade.
   d. increases output.

2. Arbitrage 仲裁 · 套利
   a. makes price discrimination possible.
   b. takes advantage of price differences for the same good in different markets by buying low in one market and selling high in another market.
   c. increases the profits from price discrimination.
   d. All of the answers are correct.

3. A price discriminator charges a
   a. higher price to customers with a more inelastic demand.
   b. single price to all customers.
   c. lower price to customers with a more inelastic demand.
   d. higher price to customers with a more elastic demand.

4. Price discrimination
   a. is selling the same product at different prices to different customers.
   b. is selling different quality goods to different customers at the same price.
   c. requires that customers be able to resell the product.
   d. requires that all customers have the same demand for the product.

5. Perfect price discriminators
   a. maximize gains from trade.
   b. reduce quantity sold in the market.
   c. charge all customers a very high price.
   d. restrict output compared to competition.

Figure 14.5

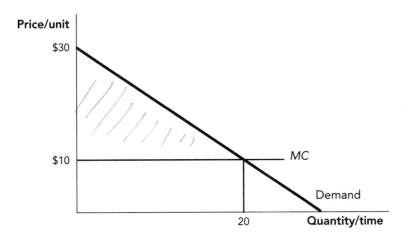

6. If the firm in Figure 14.5 is a perfect price discriminator, then the gains from trade will be
    a. $0.
    b. $200.
    c. $400.
    d. $800.

$$(30-10) \times 20 \times \frac{1}{2}$$
$$= 20 \times 20 \times \frac{1}{2}$$
$$= \$200$$

7. If the firm in Figure 14.5 is a perfect price discriminator, then the deadweight loss associated with perfect price discrimination will be
    a. $0.
    b. $200.
    c. $400.
    d. $800.

8. In economic terms price discrimination is bad if
    a. output is increased.
    b. gains from trade are increased.
    c. there is no arbitrage.
    d. None of the answers is correct.

9. With tying, the firm will sell _____ at a low price.
    a. the bundle of products
    b. the variable product
    c. the base product
    d. each individual product

10. Tying is a form of price discrimination because

    a. the base product price is set high.

    b. the variable product lets each customer reveal his or her own willingness to pay for the tied products.

    c. the variable product price is set low.

    d. the base product shows willingness to pay on the part of the customer.

Table 14.3

	Maximum willingness to pay for A&E	Maximum willingness to pay for ESPN	Price Rev	Bundle Rev
Maddux	$60	$30	$60	$80
Kaitlin	$10	$70	$70	$80
			$130	$160

11. In Table 14.3, if the provider prices A&E at $60 and ESPN at $70, then the firm will have a revenue of

    a. $0.

    b. $70.

    c. $130.

    d. $170.

12. In Table 14.3, if the provider prices A&E at $60 and ESPN at $70, then

    a. Kaitlin will buy A&E but not ESPN, and Maddux will buy ESPN but not A&E.

    b. both Kaitlin and Maddux will buy A&E and ESPN.

    c. Kaitlin will buy ESPN but not A&E, and Maddux will buy A&E but not ESPN.

    d. neither Kaitlin nor Maddux will buy either channel.

13. In Table 14.3, if the provider bundles A&E and ESPN at a price of $80, then the firm will have revenue of

    a. $0.

    b. $80.

    c. $160.

    d. $170.

14. In Table 14.3, if the provider bundles A&E and ESPN at a price of $80, then

    a. Kaitlin will buy the bundle but not Maddux.

    b. Maddux will buy the bundle but not Kaitlin.

    c. Kaitlin and Maddux will both buy the bundle.

    d. neither Kaitlin nor Maddux will buy the bundle.

15. Bundling

    a. makes customers buy a low-quality product to get a high-quality one.

    b. reduces output.

    c. makes customers buy something they do not like to get a good they do like.

    d. is a form of price discrimination.

Answers to Self-Practice Questions

1. a, Topic: Price Discrimination

2. b, Topic: Price Discrimination

3. a, Topic: Price Discrimination

4. a, Topic: Price Discrimination

5. a, Topic: Price Discrimination

6. b, Topic: Price Discrimination

7. a, Topic: Price Discrimination

8. d, Topic: Is Price Discrimination Bad?

9. c, Topic: Tying and Bundling

10. b, Topic: Tying and Bundling

11. c, Topic: Tying and Bundling

12. c, Topic: Tying and Bundling

13. c, Topic: Tying and Bundling

14. c, Topic: Tying and Bundling

15. d, Topic: Tying and Bundling

15

Cartels, Oligopolies, and Monopolistic Competition

Learning Objectives

This chapter covers markets that fall between competitive markets and monopolies. The topics covered in this chapter include:

> Cartels

> Oligopolies

> Monopolistic Competition

> The Economics of Advertising

Summary

An industry that is dominated by a small number of firms an **oligopoly**. A **cartel** is a group of suppliers who try to act as if they were a monopoly. If successful, cartel members can increase industry profits by agreeing to decrease industry output, which leads to a higher price for the product.

Cartels generally are not long lasting for three reasons. The first reason is that members of a cartel each have an incentive to cheat on the cartel agreement. A second cause of cartel instability is new entrants and demand responses. The third reason for cartels breaking down is government prosecution in areas where cartels are illegal.

The incentive that cartel members have to cheat on the cartel agreement to reduce output can be seen in Table 15.1, where each dollar figure is the oil revenues of each country (Russia is R and Saudi Arabia is SA) in millions of dollars.

Notice that the best the industry can do, collectively, is to cooperate and make industry revenue of $1 billion, compared to $900 million, if either country cheats on the cartel agreement while the other keeps to it; and $800 million if both countries cheat on the cartel agreement. Even though cheating reduces industry revenues, each country has an incentive to cheat on the agreement.

A **dominant strategy** is a strategy that has a higher payoff than any other, no matter what the other party does. In Table 15.1, each country's dominant strategy is to cheat on the agreement. If the two countries cooperate, both earn $500 million in revenue. If Russia cheats on the agreement, Russia makes $600 million in revenue, which is more than it would make, if it cooperated and Saudi Arabia also cooperated. And if Saudi Arabia cheats, Russia makes more revenue ($400 million) by cheating too. By cheating, Russia makes $400 million compared to the $300 million it would have made by cooperating while Saudi Arabia cheated. Thus, Russia's dominant strategy is to cheat, because Russia makes more revenue no matter what Saudi Arabia does. The analysis is the same for Saudi Arabia, whose dominant strategy is also to cheat no matter what Russia does.

Table 15.1

		Russia's strategies	
		Cooperate	**Cheat** For SA
Saudi Arabia's	**Cooperate**	$500 for each	$300 R, $600 SA
strategies	**Cheat**	$600 SA, $300 R	$400 for each

Notice that this incentive to cheat causes the cartel members to jointly make the lowest revenue, $800 million, when both cheat, compared to the $900 million they would make if only one country cheats on the cartel. The cartel members could make $1 billion, if they both cooperated and lived up to the cartel agreement. A situation like this is known as the **prisoner's dilemma,** in which the pursuit of individual interest leads to a group outcome that is in the interest of no one. In this example, both parties cheat, thereby reducing group and individual country income, which is in the interest of neither country.

Cartels might be successful to the extent that the reasons why they are not long lasting are absent. The incentive to cheat is always there. If the cartel is in the production of a natural resource that is found in only a limited number of places, then new entrants and demand responses may be limited. Of course, even with a resource like oil, OPEC (Organization of the Petroleum Exporting Countries) is a cartel that led to more production, as people searched for oil in new places, and to more demand responses, as people found substitutes. Similarly, in the example of diamonds, the cartel has encouraged the production of man-made diamonds. Finally, to the extent that government regulation and prosecution are absent, cartels may be more stable.

Of course, with many of the resource cartels, not only is there an absence of government prosecution, governments are also responsible for creating and sponsoring the cartels. A single government cartel, such as U.S. milk regulations, is more stable and puts the interest of a particular group, suppliers, ahead of the interest of society, including consumers. With a single-government cartel, those cheating on the cartel may be prosecuted, reducing the incentive of members to cheat. This type of cartel is a serious problem in poor countries like Mexico, Russia, Indonesia, and many African countries.

For government-sponsored natural resource cartels across several countries, for example, OPEC, the incentive to cheat is still there. Government cartel members may even dislike each other enough to go to war with each other. Such cartels may have more limited success than government-sponsored cartels in one country.

As we have seen, firms in an oligopoly are unlikely to be able to produce the joint profit-maximizing quantity. These firms are also unlikely to produce as much as they would in a highly competitive market. So prices in an oligopoly tend to be below monopoly prices, but above competitive prices.

Monopolistically competitive firms sell similar but differentiated products. Because their product is differentiated, the firms face a downward-sloping demand for their product. But because their products are still somewhat similar, these firms earn zero economic profits or a normal profit in the long run.

Advertising can serve several functions. Advertising can be informative as in advertising about product price, quality, and availability. It can also change what the product means to the consumer, adding to a consumer's understanding and enjoyment of a product.

Key Terms

oligopoly a market dominated by a small number of firms

cartel a group of suppliers that tries to act as if they were a monopoly

monopolistic competition a market with many firms, each of whom face a downward-sloping demand curve but earn zero or normal profits on average.

strategic decision making decision making in interactive situations

dominant strategy a strategy that has a higher payoff than any other strategy, no matter what the other player does

prisoner's dilemma situations in which the pursuit of individual interest leads to a group outcome that is in no one's interest

antitrust laws laws that give the government the power to regulate or prohibit business practices that may be anticompetitive

Traps, Hints, and Reminders

Cartel members have an incentive to cheat on their agreement.

The incentive to cheat on a cartel agreement can lead to a prisoner's dilemma, in which members acting in their own interest, results in an outcome that is not in the interest of any single firm.

Government cartels put the interest of a group (that is, suppliers) above the interest of society in general and buyers in particular.

Homework Quiz

1. A cartel is a group of suppliers that try to act
   a. in the public interest.
   b. as if it were a network.
   c. as if it were a monopoly.
   d. All of the answers are correct.

2. Cartels tend to collapse due to
   a. government sponsorship.
   b. cheating by members.
   c. a lack of entry of new members.
   d. All of the answers are correct.

3. Cartels have a better chance of stability when the
   a. government sponsors the cartel rather than prosecutes its members.
   b. members cheat on the agreement.
   c. profit made encourages entry.
   d. All of the answers are correct.

4. The prisoner's dilemma leads to an outcome that is
   a. best for one member of the group.
   b. in the interest of no one in the group.
   c. optimal for all members of the group.
   d. in the interest of all but the leading member of the group.

5. A dominant strategy is one that leads to
   a. a dominant payoff for the group collectively.
   b. the party with the dominant strategy dominating other cartel members.
   c. a government-sponsored cartel.
   d. a higher payoff for one party regardless of what the other party does.

Table 15.2

		Russia's Strategies	
		Cooperate	**Cheat**
Mexico's	**Cooperate**	$300 for each	$100 M, $400 R
strategies	**Cheat**	$400 M, $100 R	$200 for each

6. In Table 15.2, the best the two countries can do jointly is
   a. to cooperate.
   b. to have Russia cheat, while Mexico cooperates.
   c. to have Russia cooperate, while Mexico cheats.
   d. to cheat.

7. In Table 15.2, Russia's dominant strategy is to

    a. do what Mexico does.

    b. do the opposite of what Mexico does.

    c. cooperate.

    d. cheat.

8. In Table 15.2, if both countries follow their dominant strategy, their combined revenues will then be

    a. $200.

    b. $400.

    c. $600.

    d. None of the answers is correct.

9. In Table 15.2, a way for the two countries to get to the best joint revenue result is to

    a. compete.

    b. form a cartel and cooperate.

    c. form a cartel and cheat.

    d. encourage entry.

10. Laws that give the government power to regulate or prohibit business practices that may be anticompetitive are known as

    a. monopolistic competition.

    b. cartels.

    c. antitrust.

    d. the prisoner's dilemma.

11. Firms in monopolistically competitive industries face demand curves that are

    a. horizontal.

    b. vertical.

    c. upward sloping.

    d. downward sloping.

12. Monopolistically competitive firms earn zero or normal economic profits

    a. in the short run.

    b. in the long run.

    c. always.

    d. never.

13. Informative advertising

    a. is part of the good.

    b. persuades people to buy the good.

    c. gives the consumer information like price and availability.

    d. All of the answers are correct.

14. Advertising can

    a. provide information such as price and availability.

    b. inform the consumer about the product.

    c. be part of what the consumer consumes with the product.

    d. All of the answers are correct.

15. Oligopoly price tends to be

    a. higher than the monopoly price.

    b. equal to the monopoly price.

    c. lower than the monopoly price.

    d. set by the government.

Self-Practice Questions

1. With a government–sponsored cartel, the government is

    a. considering the interests of the suppliers and consumers equally.

    b. putting the interest of consumers ahead of the group of suppliers.

    c. putting the public interest first.

    d. putting the interest of the group of suppliers ahead of consumers.

2. An oligopoly is a market

    a. with many competitors.

    b. with a single firm.

    c. with a few firms.

    d. controlled by the government.

3. Antitrust is

    a. when consumers do not trust the product a firm produces.

    b. laws that give the government the power to regulate or prohibit business practices that may be anticompetitive.

    c. when firms in a cartel do not trust each other and thus reach an outcome that is in no firm's best interest.

    d. informal rules firms use to enforce cartel agreements.

4. Cartels

    a. are permanent.

    b. tend to be very stable.

    c. tend to lose their power and collapse.

    d. are never able to affect industry profits.

5. Cartels are often formed in natural resources like diamonds or oil because

    a. the incentive to cheat is less in these products.

    b. others without the natural resource cannot enter the market.

    c. governments cannot prosecute cartel members in such industries.

    d. All of the answers are correct.

6. The prisoner's dilemma is that in which, whether participants are guilty or not, the dominant strategy is to

a. confess. 承认，坦白

b. not confess.

c. escape.

d. not talk to the police at all.

Table 15.2

		Canada's strategies	
		Cooperate	**Cheat**
Venezuela's strategies	**Cooperate**	$250 for each	$50 V, $400 C
	Cheat	$400 V, $50 C	$150 for each

7. In Table 15.2, the best the two countries can do jointly is

a. to both cooperate. 共同地.

b. for Canada to cheat, while Venezuela cooperates.

c. for Canada to cooperate, while Venezuela cheats.

d. to both cheat.

8. In Table 15.2, Venezuela's dominant strategy is to

a. do what Canada does.   TC 约 67

b. do the opposite of what Canada does.

c. cooperate.

d. cheat.

9. In Table 15.2, if both countries follow their dominant strategy, then their combined revenues will be

a. $300.

b. $450.   400+50

c. $500.

d. None of the answers is correct.

10. In Table 15.2, a way for the two countries to get to the best joint revenue result is to

a. compete.

b. form a cartel and cooperate.

c. form a cartel and cheat.

d. encourage entry.

11. Firms in monopolistically competitive industries sell
    a. complementary products.
    b. similar products.
    c. identical products.
    d. products by advertising.

12. Monopolistically competitive firms
    a. lose money in the short run.
    b. earn economic profits in the long run.
    c. earn zero economic profits in the short run.
    d. earn zero economic profits in the long run.

13. Information advertising includes information on
    a. the lifestyle of people who use the product.
    b. the price or quantity of the product.
    c. the famous people who use the product.
    d. All of theanswers are correct.

14. Advertising can be
    a. informative.
    b. persuasive.
    c. part of what the consumer consumes with the product.
    d. All of the answers are correct.

15. Oligopoly output tends to be
    a. greater than the monopoly output.
    b. equal to the monopoly output.
    c. less than the monopoly output.
    d. more stable than the monopoly output.

Answers to Self-Practice Questions

1. d, Topic: Cartels

2. c, Topic: Cartels

3. b, Topic: Cartels

4. c, Topic: Cartels

5. b, Topic: Cartels

6. a, Topic: Oligopolies

7. a, Topic: Oligopolies

8. d, Topic: Oligopolies

9. a, Topic: Oligopolies

10. b, Topic: Oligopolies

11. b, Topic: Monopolistic Competition

12. d, Topic: Monopolistic Competition

13. b, Topic: The Economics of Advertising

14. d, Topic: The Economics of Advertising

15. a, Topic: The Economics of Advertising

16

Competing for Monopoly: The Economics of Network Goods

Learning Objectives

This chapter covers network goods, such as Facebook or Match.com, that are more valuable to people the more users there are. The topics covered include:

> Network Goods Are Usually Sold by Monopolies or Oligopolies
> The "Best" Products May Not Always Win
> Standard Wars Are Common
> Competition "For the Market" Instead of "In the Market"
> Contestable Markets
> Antitrust and Network Goods
> Music Is a Network Good

Summary

A **network good** is a good whose value to one consumer increases the more other consumers use that good. Examples include Internet message board and fax machines. Most people enjoy posting on a message board when other people also post on the same message board, and there is interaction among members.

Network goods are usually sold by monopolies or oligopolies (an oligopoly is a market dominated by a small number of firms). Standards wars are common when a market for network goods is first being established. When networks are important, the "best" product may not always be the winner. Competition in the market for network goods is "for the market" instead of "in the market."

The "best" product may not always win because the standards war may be a coordination game that results in a Nash equilibrium, in which a version of the good that is not the best (or later becomes not the best as innovation takes place) is used. A **coordination game** is one in which the players are better off if they choose the same strategies rather than different strategies, but there is also more than one strategy to potentially coordinate. A **Nash equilibrium** is a situation in which no player has an incentive to change his or her strategy unilaterally. For example, Microsoft Windows may not be the "best" operating system, but most users have no incentive to change to another system and thus make their computer incompatible with those of most other users in the world.

The monopoly or oligopoly problem with network goods is mitigated if the market is contestable. A **contestable market** is one a competitor could credibly enter and then take away business from the incumbent. Contestable markets are those in which the fixed costs of market entry are low compared to potential revenue, there are few or no legal barriers to entry, the incumbent firm has no unique or hard-to-replicate resource, and consumers are open to the prospect of dealing with a new competitor in the field. The history of the spreadsheet program market shows that competition for the market can cause changes in the standard network good; for example, domination in the spreadsheet market has moved from VisiCalc to Lotus 1-2-3 to Quattro Pro to Excel over time.

Switching costs are the costs of switching purchases from one firm to another. Incumbent firms sometimes try to raise switching costs to reduce competition for their customers.

Key Terms

network good a good whose value to one consumer increases the more other consumers use the good

Nash equilibrium a situation in which no player has an incentive to change his or her strategy unilaterally

coordination game a game in which players are better off if they choose the same strategies rather than different strategies; there is, however, more than one strategy to potentially coordinate

contestable market a market in which a competitor could credibly enter and then take away business from the incumbent

switching costs the costs of switching purchases from one firm to another; firms sometimes try to raise switching costs to reduce competition for their customers

Traps, Hints, and Reminders

With a network good, the competition is more *for* the market more than it is among goods *in* the market.

With a network good, the "best" good does not necessarily win the competition for the market, but competition for the market still means that the dominant network good can change.

Homework Quiz

1. A network good is one

  a. that must be consumed with another good.

  b. whose value to one consumer increases the more other consumers use the good.

  c. that is complementary to other goods.

  d. All of the answers are correct.

2. Network goods

  a. are usually sold by competitive firms.

  b. commonly have standards wars in establishing networks.

  c. are always the best possible product.

  d. All of the answers are correct.

3. Network goods

  a. are usually sold by monopolies or oligopolies.

  b. have competition *in* the market not *for* the market.

  c. are the winning goods.

  d. All of the answers are correct.

4. A Nash equilibrium is a situation in which

  a. the optimum result is achieved.

  b. the competitive optimum is achieved.

  c. no player has an incentive to change his or her strategy unilaterally.

  d. All of the answers are correct.

5. A network good may lead to other than the best product being adopted if consumers

  a. are irrational.

  b. reach a Nash equilibrium at a product other than the best product.

  c. pick competing goods.

  d. want to be among a small group of exclusive users of the good.

6. With a network good

  a. the standard never changes.

  b. the standard can change as improved versions of the good are developed.

  c. the standard changes frequently.

  d. no standard is adopted.

7. A coordination game

  a. is one in which the players are better off if they choose the same strategies.

  b. is one in which there is more than one strategy on which to potentially coordinate.

  c. can lead to other than the best possible network good being adopted.

  d. All of the answers are correct.

8. Contestable markets are

   a. markets that a competitor could credibly enter and take away business from the incumbent.

   b. markets with many competitors.

   c. markets set up by the government.

   d. organized markets like stock exchanges.

9. Contestable markets have

   a. low or no legal barriers to entry.

   b. low fixed entry costs compared to potential revenue.

   c. customers who are open to dealing with a new competitor.

   d. All of the answers are correct.

10. Contestable markets have

    a. high legal barriers to entry.

    b. high fixed entry costs compared to potential revenue.

    c. no unique or hard-to-replicate resource that is available only to the incumbent firm.

    d. All of the answers are correct.

11. An example of a network good would be

    a. software program like Microsoft Word.

    b. a self-defense skill like karate.

    c. a dress a woman would wear to a Mardi Gras ball.

    d. None of the answers is correct.

12. Switching costs are

    a. the costs of getting your good to market.

    b. advertising costs.

    c. the costs of consumers switching purchases from one firm to another.

    d. the costs of identifying new consumers.

13. Firms sometime try to raise switching costs by

    a. loyalty programs.

    b. bulk shipping.

    c. doing nothing; firms only want to lower costs.

    d. advertising more.

14. The more contestable a market

    a. the greater switching costs are.

    b. the greater the incentive for product improvement is.

    c. the longer a standard will last.

    d. the less likely there will be entry in the market.

15. A standard for a network good will last a longer time if the market

    a. is easily contestable.

    b. is a cooperative game.

    c. has low switching costs.

    d. is not easily contestable.

Self-Practice Questions

1. A network good is one

    a. that requires other goods to work.

    b. whose value to the consumer comes from being an exclusive user.

    c. whose value to the consumer increases as more consumers use it.

    d. that is a complete network in itself.

2. Network goods

    a. are usually sold by competitive firms.

    b. have competition *in* the market not *for* the market.

    c. may not lead to the best version of the product winning the market.

    d. All of the answers are correct.

3. Network goods

    a. are usually sold by monopolies or oligopolies.

    b. engage in competition *for* the market not *in* the market.

    c. may not lead to the best version of the product winning the market.

    d. All of the answers are correct.

4. An example of a network good is

    a. a candy bar.

    b. Facebook.

    c. a shirt.

    d. None of the answers is correct.

5. A coordination game is one in which

    a. the players are better off if they choose the same strategies.

    b. there is only one strategy on which to potentially coordinate.

    c. the best possible network good gets to be adopted.

    d. All of the answers are correct.

6. A Nash equilibrium in a network good

   a. is always optimal.

   b. is illegal.

   c. may be for a standard that is no longer optimal.

   d. leads to a competitive outcome.

7. Contestable markets have

   a. high legal barriers to entry.

   b. low fixed entry costs compared to potential revenue.

   c. customers who are not open to dealing with a new competitor.

   d. All of the answers are correct.

8. Contestable markets have

   a. low legal barriers to entry.

   b. high fixed entry costs compared to potential revenue.

   c. a unique or hard-to-replicate resource available only to the incumbent firm.

   d. All of the answers are correct.

9. If customers in a network good reach a Nash equilibrium, then

   a. the market is competitive.

   b. output is optimal.

   c. the standard product may not be the best available product.

   d. All of the answers are correct.

10. To deal with contestability, firms try to

   a. lower advertising costs.

   b. raise advertising costs.

   c. lower switching costs.

   d. raise switching costs.

11. The lower the switching costs,

   a. the cheaper the product.

   b. the higher the price of the product.

   c. the more contestable the market.

   d. the longer a standard will last.

12. With network goods,

   a. there is little competition.

   b. there is a lot of competition in the market.

   c. there is a lot of competition for the market.

   d. the government should set the price.

13. With a network good,

    a. the standard is set by the government and rarely changes.

    b. the standard can change frequently if switching costs are high.

    c. the standard can change frequently if customers are open to new producers.

    d. no standard is adopted.

14. Network markets can be highly competitive if

    a. the good is produced by monopolies or oligopolies.

    b. the market is contestable.

    c. switching costs are high.

    d. All of the answers are correct.

15. Markets for network goods

    a. always adopt the best version of the network good.

    b. are always competitive.

    c. may not adopt the best version of the network good.

    d. have high switching costs.

Answers to Self-Practice Questions

1. c, Topic: Network Goods
2. c, Topic: Network Goods
3. d, Topic: Network Goods
4. b, Topic: Network Goods
5. a, Topic: Network Goods
6. c, Topic: Network Goods
7. b, Topic: Network Goods
8. a, Topic: Contestable Markets
9. c, Topic: Network Goods
10. d, Topic: Contestable Markets
11. c, Topic: Contestable Markets
12. c, Topic: Network Goods
13. c, Topic: Network Goods
14. b, Topic: Contestable Markets
15. c, Topic: Network Goods

17

Labor Markets

Learning Objectives

In this chapter you will learn about labor markets. Since labor is a factor of production the market for labor is conceptually different than regular output markets. The topics covered are:

> The Demand for Labor and the Marginal Product of Labor
> Supply of Labor
> Labor Market Issues
> How Bad Is Labor Market Discrimination, or Can Lakisha Catch a Break?

Summary

Labor is the key good in the economy for most of us. The amount of time that we work and the price or wage we get for working determines how many goods we get to consume.

A worker is worth what he or she contributes to the firm. What a worker contributes can be measured by the **marginal product of labor (MPL)**. The MPL is the increase in a firm's revenues created by hiring an additional worker. If a lawn service mows 12 lawns a day, at $20 per lawn, hires another worker and then is able to mow 14 lawns per day, then the MPL of the last worker hired is $40.

Consider the data in Table 17.1.

Table 17.1

Number of workers	Lawns mowed @ $20 per lawn	Marginal product of labor (MPL) for the last worker hired
One	4	$80
Two	9	$100
Three	12	$60
Four	14	$40

When the firm hires one worker, the worker mows 4 lawns a day and, at $20 per lawn, has a MPL of $80. When the firm hires the second worker, the two workers are able to mow 9 lawns total or 5 additional lawns a day, so the MPL of the second worker is 5 lawns times $20 per lawn or $100. The third worker increases the number of lawns mowed per day by 3 and thus has an MPL of $60. The fourth worker is the example from the previous paragraph and has an MPL of 2 lawns times $20, and thus has an MPL of $40.

Firms want to hire those workers who cost them less than they contribute to the firm. If the firm in Table 17.1 must pay its workers $7 per hour during an 8-hour day, then each worker costs them $56 per day. Under these conditions the firm will want to hire workers 1-3, who each contribute more than $56 to the firm, and not a fourth worker, who would contribute only $40 to the firm. If, on the other hand, the firm must pay its workers $8 per hour for an 8-hour day, then each worker costs the firm $64 per day and the firm will want to hire workers 1 and 2, who contribute more to the firm than $64. But the firm will not want to hire the third and fourth workers, who each contribute less than $64 to the firm.

It is important to understand that the first hires are not necessarily "better" workers. Firms have the first worker hired do the most productive work. In our example, the first cuts the easiest lawns with the fewest steep slopes and fewest trees and other obstacles to work around. As other workers are subsequently hired, the firm gives them less productive tasks. In our example; they do yards that are more time intensive. So it may not matter in what order workers are hired, the later-hired workers will still have a lower MPL.

The MPL is the demand curve for labor and is downward sloping as usual. The market supply curve for labor is upward sloping as usual. This means higher wages lead to more work. Some individuals might work less if they are paid a higher wage, but the higher wage will attract other workers into the labor market.

The labor market is shown by Figure 17.1.

In Figure 17.1 the equilibrium wage is W_e, and the equilibrium number of workers hired is N_e, where the supply of labor equals the MPL or the demand for labor.

Workers in low-skilled jobs in a developed country like the United States tend to make more than workers doing the same job in a less-developed country like India. This is because the workers in the less-developed country work in a less-productive economy and thus have lower MPL than workers doing the same job in a more productive economy.

Figure 17.1

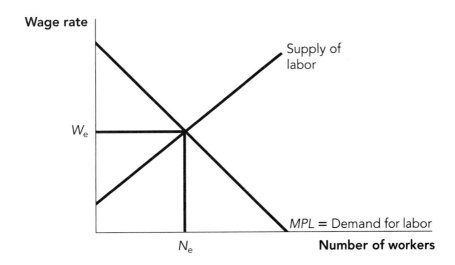

Human capital is the tools of the mind, the stuff in people's heads that makes them productive. It is not something we are born with—it is accumulated through investing time and other resources in education, training, and experience. Education is related to higher lifetime earnings. The return on education has grown over the last 60 years.

Some jobs pay more because they involve more risk or require workers to perform unpleasant tasks (or work in unpleasant circumstances). These differences in pay are called compensating differentials. A **compensating differential** is a difference in wages that offsets differences in working conditions. Similar jobs must have similar compensation packages. If a fun job paid more than a job that was only a little fun, then everyone would want the fun job, driving down its wage, and few people would want the job with little fun, driving up its wage. This is how the market creates compensating differentials.

Workers in wealthier countries can use that wealth to buy lower levels of risk. This leads to a death rate of Chinese coal miners that is 100 times higher than the rate for U.S. coal miners.

Unions raise wages by reducing the supply of workers for a particular job. This is shown in Figure 17.2. In the figure, the union reduces the supply of workers, shifting it up and to the left. This causes the equilibrium wage to rise from W_1 to W_2 for those workers employed. But notice that the amount of employment declines from N_1 to N_2. Unions can also possibly reduce wages over time if they slow growth in productivity. Finally, not all unions call themselves unions. Professional associations, such as those for accountants or lawyers, restrict access to jobs and thus lead to an increase in wages as would be the case with any other union.

There is discrimination in the labor market. Some discrimination is good; for example, we would like our hospitals; to discriminate regarding who they let operate on us. Some discrimination, however, is bad, if it is associated with characteristics that do not affect job performance.

There are two overall types of discrimination that can be bad. One is **statistical discrimination**, which uses information about group averages to make conclusions about individuals. An example of this would be asking very tall individuals about bas-

Figure 17.2

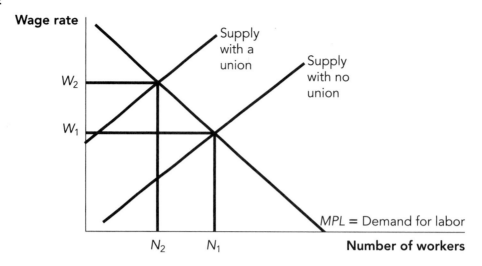

ketball based on only knowing their height. Profit-seeking business owners, who can make money finding the best workers, tend to reduce and can eliminate statistical discrimination in labor markets.

Preference-based discrimination is the second type of discrimination discussed in the textbook. There are three subdivisions of preference-based discrimination—employer discrimination, customer discrimination, and employee discrimination.

Employer discrimination, like statistical discrimination, is reduced and can be eliminated by market forces. The nondiscriminating will be able to hire the discriminated-against workers more cheaply and compete the discriminating firm out of business or at least make the discriminating employer pay a price for the discrimination. Profit-seeking employers, by hiring more of the discriminated-against workers, tend to raise their wages and reduce the wages of the favored workers by reducing the demand for them.

Customer discrimination is tougher to solve. If women will not go to a gynecologist who uses a male nurse, then those gynecologists who hire male nurses may go out of business. If you expect Asian-looking workers in the Chinese restaurants you go to, then Chinese restaurants that hire white or black servers and cooks may go out of business.

Discrimination by employees occurs when employees only want to work with a certain type of people. Like customer discrimination, employee discrimination is hard to overcome. If when you hire a mixed crew of workers, one group quits or the two groups have constant disagreements that reduce productivity, then your business will be less productive and you may even go out of business.

Of course, as groups become less distinct, customer and employee discrimination may each become less of a problem. Finally, it is important to note that governments often enforce the discriminatory preferences of their society.

Key Terms

marginal product of labor (MPL) the increase in a firm's revenues created by hiring an additional laborer

human capital tools of the mind, the stuff in people's heads that makes them productive

compensating differential a difference in wages that offsets differences in working conditions

statistical discrimination using information about group averages to make conclusions about individual

Traps, Hints, and Reminders

The marginal product of labor (MPL) is the increase in revenue a firm gets from hiring another worker.

Unions raise member wages by restricting the supply of workers.

Preference-based labor market discrimination can be due to the preferences of business owners, customers, or employees.

Human capital is the tools of the mind. It is also produced, not inborn.

Jobs may have different wages because they have different characteristics, but jobs must have similar compensation packages.

Homework Quiz

1. The marginal product of labor is the change in the firm's revenue created by
   a. producing one more unit of output.
   b. selling one more unit of output.
   c. hiring an additional worker.
   d. All of the answers are correct.

2. If a firm that charges $50 to mow a lawn can mow 2 lawns a day with 2 workers, and 5 lawns a day with 3 workers, then the marginal product of the third worker is
   a. $100
   b. $150.
   c. $250.
   d. None of the answers is correct.

3. The marginal product of workers declines as more workers are hired because
   a. the first worker is put to work on the most productive tasks.
   b. the first worker is a better worker than later hires.
   c. more workers are less efficient than fewer workers.
   d. more workers conspire to shirk their jobs.

4. Human capital is

  a. only innate abilities.

  b. acquired by investing resources in education, training, and experience.

  c. acquired by exercise and physical training.

  d. only the talents you are born with.

5. While the individual labor supply might be backward-bending, the market labor supply curve is positively sloped because higher wages

  a. make people wealthier.

  b. encourage people to take more leisure time.

  c. encourage businesses to hire more workers.

  d. encourage more people to enter the labor market.

6. Compensating differentials are

  a. a form of labor market discrimination.

  b. differences in working conditions.

  c. differences in wages that offset differences in working conditions.

  d. a form of human capital.

7. Statistical discrimination is using information about

  a. an individual to draw conclusions about a group.

  b. an individual to draw conclusions about that individual.

  c. group averages to draw conclusions about individuals.

  d. group averages to draw conclusions about the group.

8. The market may compete away employer discrimination by making

  a. discrimination profitable.

  b. discriminating firms less profitable.

  c. discrimination illegal.

  d. discrimination impossible.

9. A firm will hire workers so long as

  a. the marginal product of labor is falling.

  b. increased revenue from hiring an extra worker is less than the wage.

  c. increased revenue from hiring an extra worker is greater than the wage.

  d. the wage rate does not rise.

10. If you see a disproportionate number of female workers in a job, then you know

  a. the customers of the firm are engaging in customer discrimination.

  b. the employer is engaging in hiring discrimination.

  c. the employees are engaging in employee discrimination.

  d. None of the answers is correct.

Table 17.2

Number of workers	Houses cleaned @ $100 per house	Marginal product of labor (MPL) for the last worker hired
Two	3	
Three	8	
Four	11	
Five	13	

11. In Table 17.2, the marginal product of labor (MPL) of the fourth worker is
    a. 3 houses.
    b. $300.
    c. $11,000.
    d. 11 houses.

12. In Table 17.2, the marginal product of labor (MPL) of the fifth worker is
    a. 2 houses.
    b. $200.
    c. $13,000.
    d. 13 houses.

13. Among the following jobs, the one you would expect to pay the least is
    a. construction laborer.
    b. order taker in a fast food restaurant.
    c. laborer for a lawn service business.
    d. clerk in a CD store.

14. Workers in a poor country earn less than workers in similar jobs in a rich country because their wages are lower due to
    a. exploitation.
    b. the low productivity of many other sectors in their economy.
    c. discrimination.
    d. capitalism, particularly human capital.

15. Jobs tend to pay more when
    a. they are more fun.
    b. they entail more responsibility.
    c. the work environment is very pleasant.
    d. All of the answers are correct.

Self-Practice Questions

1. The change in the firm's revenue created by hiring an additional worker is

   a. average cost.

   b. marginal cost.

   c. marginal product of labor.

   d. labor market discrimination.

2. If a firm that charges $1,000 to paint a house can paint 3 houses a week with 4 workers and 5 houses a week with 5 workers, then the marginal product of the fifth worker is

   a. $500.

   b. $1,000.

   c. $2,000.

   d. None of the answers is correct.

3. Human capital is

   a. tools owned by people rather than corporations.

   b. tools of the mind.

   c. tools that human workers use on a job.

   d. tools owned by the government rather than corporations.

4. Workers in a rich country earn more than workers in a poor country because workers in the rich country benefit from

   a. scarcity of capital.

   b. the productivity of many other sectors in their economy.

   c. exploiting poor countries.

   d. protectionism.

5. More education is associated with

   a. higher lifetime wages.

   b. less productivity.

   c. reduced lifetime wages due to a delay in beginning working life.

   d. reduced lifetime production.

6. Jobs tend to pay more

   a. the safer the environment is that the work is performed in.

   b. the more unpleasant the tasks are that are involved with it.

   c. the more fun they are.

   d. All of the answers are correct.

7. When you use information about a group to draw conclusions about individuals in the group, you are engaging in

a. employer discrimination.

b. statistical discrimination.

c. preference-based discrimination.

d. customer discrimination.

8. The type of discrimination the market may make less profitable and compete away is

a. government discrimination.

b. employee discrimination.

c. employer discrimination.

d. All of the answers are correct.

9. As long as the increased revenue from hiring another worker is greater than the wage, a firm will

a. hire more workers.

b. reduce its workforce.

c. raise its wage rate.

d. lower its wage rate.

10. If you see a disproportionate number of male workers in a job, then you know

a. the customers of the firm are engaging in customer discrimination.

b. the employer is engaging in hiring discrimination.

c. the employees are engaging in employee discrimination.

d. None of the answers is correct.

Table 17.3

Number of workers	Driveways repaved @ $300 per driveway	Marginal product of labor (MPL) for the last worker hired
Two	5	
Three	7	
Four	11	
Five	13	

11. In Table 17.3, the marginal product of labor (MPL) of the third worker is

a. 2 driveways.

b. $3,500.

c. $1,100.

d. 7 driveways.

12. In Table 17.3, the marginal product of labor (MPL) of the fourth worker is
    a. 4 driveways.
    b. $5,500.
    c. $2,200.
    d. 11 driveways.

13. The marginal product of labor declines because
    a. the first worker hired is the best.
    b. when you have several workers they start to shirk their duties.
    c. the first worker hired is put to work on the most productive tasks.
    d. All of the answers are correct.

14. Wage differences that offset differences in working conditions are
    a. unfair.
    b. required to get people to take on less pleasant jobs.
    c. illegal.
    d. All of the answers are correct.

15. Of the following jobs, the one you would expect to pay the most would be
    a. construction laborer.
    b. music store clerk.
    c. clothing store clerk.
    d. All of these jobs are unskilled and should pay the same.

Answers to Self-Practice Questions

1. c, Topic: The Demand For Labor and the Marginal Product of Labor

2. c, Topic: The Demand For Labor and the Marginal Product of Labor

3. b, Topic: Labor Market Issues

4. b, Topic: Labor Market Issues

5. a, Topic: Labor Market Issues

6. b, Topic: Labor Market Issues

7. b, Topic: How Bad Is Labor Market Discrimination, or Can Lakisha Catch a Break?

8. c, Topic: How Bad Is Labor Market Discrimination, or Can Lakisha Catch a Break?

9. a, Topic: The Demand For Labor and the Marginal Product of Labor

10. d, Topic: How Bad Is Labor Market Discrimination, or Can Lakisha Catch a Break?

11. c, Topic: The Demand For Labor and the Marginal Product of Labor

12. c, Topic: The Demand For Labor and the Marginal Product of Labor

13. c, Topic: The Demand For Labor and the Marginal Product of Labor

14. b, Topic: Labor Market Issues

15. a, Topic: Labor Market Issues

18

Public Goods and the Tragedy of the Commons

Learning Objectives

In this chapter, you learn that some goods are not traditional private goods. The topics covered are:

> Four Types of Goods
> Private Goods and Public Goods
> Nonrival Private Goods
> Common Resources and the Tragedy of the Commons

Summary

A good can either be excludable or nonexcludable. An excludable good is one that the owner can prevent others from using at a low cost. A **nonexcludable good** is one that is difficult to prevent people from using at low cost.

A good can also be either rival or nonrival. A rival good is one that one person's use of it prevents others from using the good. For example, if I eat and enjoy a candy bar, you cannot eat and enjoy that candy bar. A **nonrival good** is a good that one person's use of that good does not reduce the ability of another person to use it. For example, your watching a sunset will not reduce my ability to enjoy the same sunset.

A **free rider** enjoys the benefits of a public good without paying a share of the costs. A **forced rider** is someone who pays a share of the costs of a public good but who does not enjoy the benefits.

Private goods are rival and excludable. For example, if I eat a hamburger, then you cannot eat it, making a hamburger rival in consumption. Similarly, the owner of a hamburger can easily prevent others from using it by eating it.

Public goods are nonrival and nonexcludable. For example, if I enjoy a sunset or the national defense of the United States, that does not prevent you from enjoying either of these goods. And it is very costly to try to prevent other people from consuming a sunset or the national defense.

Advertising has made it possible for some public goods like broadcast television (TV) and radio to be produced by the market. Since everyone who watches or listens has advertisements (commercials) broadcast to them, the advertisers pay for the public good and the broadcaster provides the programming to the viewer for free.

Nonrival private goods are nonrival but excludable. For example, your watching a movie channel like HBO (Home Box Office) on cable TV will not reduce my enjoyment of it. However, cable TV companies can cheaply exclude those that do not pay for their services from receiving their programming. All they have to do, if you do not pay, is turn off their services to your house.

Common resources are rival but nonexcludable. For example, if one fisherman catches a lobster, then other fishermen cannot catch that particular lobster. Thus, lobsters are a rival good. But no one owns the lobsters. Since no one owns the lobsters in the sea, and one fisherman cannot prevent another fisherman from fishing, lobsters are nonexcludable.

Because they are not excludable, common resources often lead to the tragedy of the commons. The **tragedy of the commons** is the tendency of any resource that is not owned to be overused and undermaintained. The tragedy is that in the case of common resources, such as fisheries, the fishermen have an incentive to overuse their resource (by fishing too much) and deplete the stock of fish, thus driving their way of life (livelihood) out of existence.

Governments have tried to overcome the tragedy of the commons by command and control. However, command and control sometimes fail since firms just work harder to use more of the resource, for example, by fishing more in a limited fishing season. A more successful government approach has been to assign property rights to the resource to a limited number of producers. Then these producers, like any owner, have an incentive to maintain the resource and use it at an optimal rate.

Key Terms

nonexcludable good a good that people who do not pay for cannot be easily prevented from using

nonrival good a good that one person's use of does not reduce the ability of another person to use the same good

free rider someone who enjoys the benefits of a public good without paying a share of the costs

forced rider someone who pays a share of the costs of a public good but who does not enjoy the benefits

private goods goods that are excludable and rival

public goods goods that are nonexcludable and nonrival

nonrival private goods goods that are excludable but nonrival

common resources goods that are nonexcludable but rival

tragedy of the commons the tendency of any resource that is unowned, and hence nonexcludable, to be overused and undermaintained

Traps, Hints, and Reminders

Private goods are rival and excludable.
Public goods are nonrival and nonexcludable.
Common resources are rival but nonexcludable.
Nonrival private goods are nonrival but excludable.
Public goods like a sunset need not be produced by the government.

Homework Quiz

1. If it is difficult to prevent a person from using a good at a low cost, then the good is
   a. excludable.
   b. nonexcludable.
   c. rival. 对手，竞争者
   d. nonrival.

2. A private good is one that is
   a. rival and excludable.
   b. rival and nonexcludable.
   c. nonrival and excludable.
   d. nonrival and nonexcludable.

3. A nonrival private good is one that is
   a. rival and excludable.
   b. rival and nonexcludable.
   c. nonrival and excludable.
   d. nonrival and nonexcludable.

4. A good that is nonrival and nonexcludable is a
   a. private good.
   b. public good.
   c. common resource.
   d. nonrival private good.

5. A good that is rival and nonexcludable is a
   a. private good.
   b. public good.
   c. common resource.
   d. nonrival private good.

6. A free rider is someone who
   a. enjoys the benefits of a public good while paying a share of the costs.
   b. enjoys the benefits of a public good without paying a share of the costs.
   c. pays a share of the costs of a public good without enjoying the benefits.
   d. None of the answers is correct.

7. Someone who pays a share of the costs of a public good without enjoying the benefits is a
   a. taxpayer.
   b. free rider.
   c. forced rider.
   d. tax dodger.

8. A hamburger is an example of a
   a. private good.
   b. public good.
   c. nonrival private good.
   d. common resource.

9. Asteroid deflection is an example of a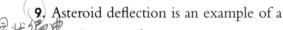
   a. private good.
   b. public good.
   c. nonrival private good.
   d. common resource.

10. Cable television is an example of a
   a. private good.
   b. public good.
   c. nonrival private good.
   d. common resource.

11. Public goods are those that are
   a. produced by the government.
   b. nonrival and nonexcludable.
   c. owned by the public.
   d. All of the answers are correct.

12. The tragedy of the commons is that common resources tend to be

    a. nonrival.

    b. overused and undermaintained.

    c. produced by the market.

    d. excludable.

13. Governments have successfully solved the tragedy of the commons by

    a. assigning the right to use the common resource.

    b. taking over the market.

    c. allowing everyone to use the resource.

    d. None of the answers is correct.

14. The animals least likely to become extinct are

    a. wild animals.

    b. those that are privately owned.

    c. those animals that are a common resource.

    d. All of the answers are correct.

15. Which animal is least likely to become extinct?

    a. bears

    b. cows

    c. whales

    d. eagles

Self-Practice Questions

1. If one person's use of a good does not reduce the ability of another person to use that good, then the good is

    a. excludable.

    b. nonexcludable.

    c. rival.

    d. nonrival.

2. A public good is one that is

    a. rival and excludable.

    b. rival and nonexcludable.

    c. nonrival and excludable.

    d. nonrival and nonexcludable

3. A common resource is one that is

    a. rival and excludable.

    b. rival and nonexcludable.

    c. nonrival and excludable.

    d. nonrival and nonexcludable.

4. A good that is rival and excludable is a

    a. private good.

    b. public good.

    c. common resource.

    d. nonrival private good.

5. A good that is nonrival and excludable is a

    a. private good.

    b. public good.

    c. common resource.

    d. nonrival private good.

6. Someone who enjoys the benefits of a public good without paying a share of its costs is a

    a. taxpayer.

    b. free rider.

    c. forced rider.

    d. tax dodger.

7. A forced rider is someone who

    a. enjoys the benefits of a public good while paying a share of its costs.

    b. enjoys the benefits of a public good without paying a share of its costs.

    c. pays the costs of a public good without enjoying the benefits.

    d. All of the answers are correct.

8. A provider of satellite TV, such as Direct TV, is an example of a

    a. private good.

    b. public good.

    c. nonrival private good.

    d. common resource.

9. A lobster in the ocean is an example of a

    a. private good.

    b. public good.

    c. nonrival private good.

    d. common resource.

10. A lobster on your plate is an example of a

    a. private good.

    b. public good.

    c. nonrival private good.

    d. common resource.

11. A sunset is an example of a

    a. private good.

    b. public good.

    c. nonrival private good.

    d. common resource.

12. Common resources

    a. tend to be undermaintained.

    b. are rival but nonexcludable.

    c. tend to be overused.

    d. All of the answers are correct.

13. What makes the tragedy of the commons a tragedy is that people who overuse their common resource will tend to

    a. make too much profit.

    b. grow too big.

    c. drive their way of life out of existence.

    d. All of the answers are correct.

14. Advertising has been used to increase the availability of

    a. nonrival private goods.

    b. private goods.

    c. common resources.

    d. All of the answers are correct.

15. Which of the following are most likely to become extinct?

    a. bears

    b. cows

    c. pigs

    d. chickens

Answers to Self-Practice Questions

1. d, Topic: Four Types of Goods

2. d, Topic: Four Types of Goods

3. b, Topic: Four Types of Goods

4. a, Topic: Four Types of Goods

5. d, Topic: Four Types of Goods

6. b, Topic: Private Goods and Public Goods

7. c, Topic: Private Goods and Public Goods

8. c, Topic: Nonrival Private Goods

9. d, Topic: Common Resources and the Tragedy of the Commons

10. a, Topic: Private Goods and Public Goods

11. b, Topic: Private Goods and Public Goods

12. d, Topic: Common Resources and the Tragedy of the Commons

13. c, Topic: Common Resources and the Tragedy of the Commons

14. a, Topic: Nonrival Private Goods

15. a, Topic: Common Resources and the Tragedy of the Commons

19

Political Economy and Public Choice

Learning Objectives

This chapter covers political economy and public choice. The topics discussed include:

> Voters and the Incentive to Be Ignorant
> Special Interests and the Incentive to Be Informed
> One Formula for Political Success: Diffuse Costs, Concentrated Benefits
> Voter Myopia and the Political Business Cycles
> Two Cheers for Democracy

Summary

This chapter begins by asking why mainstream economics is often ignored in the political realm. The authors offer three possibilities: the criticism of economics in Chapter 20 is correct, so politicians are right to ignore economic analysis; the possibility that mainstream economists are just wrong about economics; or the voting public and politicians have incentives that encourage them to ignore economics.

The first bad incentive comes from the fact that each voter knows that his or her vote is unlikely to decide a particular election. So voters individually decide not to become as informed as they might about various issues. Or voters individually decide to remain rationally ignorant. **Rational ignorance** is when the benefits from acquiring more information are less than the costs.

Rational ignorance matters because if voters are ignorant, then it is hard for them to make informed choices about what policies to support. Also, voters who are rationally ignorant will often make decisions for irrational reasons. Finally, rational ignorance matters because not everyone is rationally ignorant, and those who are not may have an advantage in getting the policies that benefit them at the expense of taxpayers as a whole.

A *special interest group* is a small group of people with a common interest. A special interest group can have an incentive to be informed. Any benefit a small group receives is spread over fewer people (a small percentage) than the voting public as a whole. Also, the benefits a special interest group can achieve for its members may, on a per member basis, be more, even much more, than the share of taxes per member that will be needed to support the government's providing the benefit.

The book discusses the U.S. sugar industry and its benefits from a government imposed quota on sugar imports. Sugar interests also donate to members of both political parties that are on the Senate Agriculture Committee who vote on the quota. In this case, sugar producers are rationally informed, since they each gain large benefits from the sugar quota and voters are rationally ignorant, since the sugar quota, costs them a cent or a few cents on any particular product that contains sugar.

The sugar example is a case of *concentrated benefits* and *diffused costs*. Concentrated benefits are benefits that accrue to a few individuals. Diffused costs are costs, like taxes, which are spread out widely, for example, like taxes, which fall on all taxpayers. Concentrated benefits and diffused costs provide an opportunity for a special interest group to get a benefit at the expense of taxpayers; they also provide an incentive to waste resources.

For example, if a policy costs society $500 and would provide a special interest group that pays 2 percent of the total tax bill of society a $400 benefit, then the group will certainly favor and push for this policy. If successful, the special interest group would then get its $400 benefit while paying $10 (or $.02 \times \$500$). So, the net gain of the special interest group is $390, that is, $400 − $10. However, society is wasting resources on this policy. It will cost society $500 to provide a $400 benefit, so $100 (or $500 − $400) is wasted. If enough policies are adopted that waste resources, then society members will see their standard of living erode.

A possible macroeconomic case of rational ignorance is that the winner of a United States presidential election can be accurately predicted by the state of the macroeconomy and the length of time the incumbent party has held the White House. This assumption is called the *political business cycle*. Maybe people in the United States who vote for president are myopic and do not consider to what extent the president is responsible for current economic conditions, or maybe the economy is the single critical issue for presidential voters. This voting pattern, of course, has created an incentive for incumbent presidents. They naturally do what they can to make the U.S. economic conditions as favorable as they can when heading into a presidential election, even if economic conditions are only artificially made to appear better. The book gives an example of social security payments being increased before a presidential election, while a tax increase was delayed until the following year. Data also shows that U.S. personal *income* has grown faster in election years than in nonelection years, and the difference is enough that it is likely not due to chance. This movement in U.S. personal income around elections is part of the political business cycle.

Up to this point in the chapter, democracy with rationally ignorant voters, special interest groups, and wasted resources does not look too good. However, when you look around the world, democratic countries are the richest, so they must be doing something right.

The alternative to democracy is often an autocratic government that seeks through control of the press to keep the people uninformed. While voters in democracies may sometimes be rationally ignorant, they are often better informed than people in auto-cratic societies, where the government controls the press. The evidence is that famines have happened not due to lack of food in a country. Rather, the reason is that the government is not responsive to the public because of a lack of a free press and representative government.

Key Terms

public choice the study of political behavior using the tools of economics

rational ignorance when the benefits of being informed are less than the costs of becoming informed

median voter theorem when voters vote for the policy that is closest to their ideal point on a line, then the ideal point of the median voter will beat any other policy in a majority rule election

Traps, Hints, and Reminders

Rational ignorance is when a person does not find it worthwhile to acquire information.

Concentrated benefits and diffused costs provide an incentive for special interest groups to be informed and may provide an incentive for the government to waste resources.

Homework Quiz

1. It is rational to remain ignorant when the costs of information are
   a. positive.
   b. negative.
   c. greater than the benefits from the information.
   d. less than the benefits from the information.

2. Among the problems created by rational ignorance is
   a. that information is more costly.
   b. that voters may decide based on irrational criteria.
   c. that old economic ideas that have been shown to be wrong.
   d. microeconomics.

3. Special interest groups can get gains for their members if
   a. benefits and costs are concentrated.
   b. benefits and costs are diffuse.
   c. benefits are concentrated and costs are diffuse.
   d. benefits are diffuse and costs are concentrated.

Use Scenario 1 to answer Questions 4 through 7.

Scenario 1

A. The interest group pays 5 percent of all taxes.

B. The interest group can get a $500 benefit from the government.

C. The policy benefit given the interest group costs the government $700.

4. In Scenario 1, the part of the benefit cost paid by members of the special interest group is
   a. $35.
   b. $465.
   c. $500.
   d. $700.

5. In Scenario 1, the net benefit to the members of the special interest group is
   a. $35.
   b. $465.
   c. $500.
   d. $700.

6. In Scenario 1, the net benefit to society is
   a. −$200 (minus $200).
   b. $35.
   c. $665.
   d. $700.

7. If the government in Scenario 1 adopts this policy, it will be
   a. maximizing societal happiness.
   b. wasting resources.
   c. rationally ignorant.
   d. maximizing GDP.

8. Famines are least likely when the press is
   a. free under a dictator.
   b. government-controlled in a democracy.
   c. free in a democracy.
   d. government-controlled under a dictator.

9. The median voter theorem says that if voters vote for the policy closest to their ideal point, then in a majority rule election
   a. the median policy will beat any other policy.
   b. the ideal point of the median voter will beat any other policy.
   c. the ideal point furthest from the median voter will beat any other policy.
   d. All of the answers are correct.

10. Special interest groups seek _____ for their members.

   a. concentrated costs

   b. diffused benefits

   c. concentrated benefits

   d. All of the answers are correct.

Self-Practice Questions

1. If the costs of information are greater than the benefits in an area, it is rational to

   a. become informed.

   b. not buy the product in that area.

   c. remain ignorant.

   d. forget the information.

2. When voters use irrational criteria, for example, the physical attractiveness of a candidate, to make a voting decision, it could be due to

   a. informed rationality.

   b. rational certainty.

   c. rational ignorance.

   d. All of the answers are correct.

3. If benefits are concentrated and costs are diffuse, then special interest groups

   a. are ineffective.

   b. can make their members better off at the expense of society as a whole.

   c. will make their members and society as a whole better off.

   d. are illegal.

Use Scenario 1 to answer Questions 4 through 7.

Scenario 1

   A. The interest group pays 10 percent of all taxes.

   B. The interest group can get a $700 benefit from the government.

   C. The policy benefit given the interest group costs the government $1,000.

4. In Scenario 1, the part of the benefit cost paid by members of the special interest group is

   a. $100.

   b. $600.

   c. $700.

   d. $1,000.

5. In Scenario 1, the net benefit to the members of the special interest group is
   a. $100.
   b. $600.
   c. $700.
   d. $1,000.

6. In Scenario 1, the net benefit to society is
   a. −$300 (minus $300).
   b. $100.
   c. $600.
   d. $900.

7. If the government in Scenario 1 adopts this policy, it will be
   a. maximizing societal happiness.
   b. making a rationally ignorant decision.
   c. rewarding an interest group at the expense of the rest of society.
   d. maximizing GDP.

8. Famines are most likely when the press is
   a. free under a dictator.
   b. government-controlled in a democracy.
   c. free in a democracy.
   d. government-controlled under a dictator.

9. Democracies have a good record in
   a. not killing their own citizens.
   b. supporting property rights.
   c. economic growth.
   d. All of the answers are correct.

10. Special interest groups seek situations that have
    a. concentrated costs.
    b. diffused costs.
    c. diffused benefits.
    d. All of the answers are correct.

Answers to Self-Practice Questions

1. c, Topic: Voters and the Incentive to Be Ignorant

2. c, Topic: Voters and the Incentive to Be Ignorant

3. b, Topic: Special Interests and the Incentive to Be Informed

4. a, Topic: One Formula for Political Success: Diffuse Costs, Concentrated Benefits

5. b, Topic: One Formula for Political Success: Diffuse Costs, Concentrated Benefits

6. a, Topic: One Formula for Political Success: Diffuse Costs, Concentrated Benefits

7. c, Topic: One Formula for Political Success: Diffuse Costs, Concentrated Benefits

8. d, Topic: Two Cheers for Democracy

9. d, Topic: Two Cheers for Democracy

10. b, Topic: Two Cheers for Democracy

20

Economics, Ethics, and Public Policy

Learning Objectives

This chapter discusses the economics of ethics and economic public policies. The topics covered in this chapter are:

> The Case for Exporting Pollution and Importing Kidneys

> Exploitation

> Meddlesome Preferences

> Fair and Equal Treatment

> Cultural Goods and Paternalism

> Poverty, Inequality, and the Distribution of Income

> Who Counts? Immigration

> Economic Ethics

Summary

This chapter deals with the question of whether any and all voluntary trade or exchange should be allowed. In this book, up until this point, we have studied positive economics. **Positive economics** deals with describing, explaining, or predicting without making recommendations. An example of a positive economic statement is that if the price ceiling on human organs were allowed to rise above the current level of zero, then the quantity of human organs supplied would also rise.

Normative economics is based on recommendations or arguments about what economic policy should be; for example, what exchanges should be allowed. An example of a normative economic statement is that trade in human organs should not be allowed.

We learned in prior chapters that when the market works, free exchange leads to maximum consumer surplus plus producer surplus. To argue that such exchanges should not be allowed, a person needs a reason. This chapter discusses six such reasons, which might be viewed as criticisms of economics. Although the authors generally dismiss these reasons, they and the author of this study guide, are economists.

The first reason the authors discuss for not allowing some voluntary exchanges is exploitation, that is, the possibly that one side of a trade is exploiting the other. The authors use a human organ donation example. Is the seller exploited if he or she does 1, 2, or 3?

1. Sell a kidney for zero dollars ($0); that is, donate it.
2. Sell a kidney for $5,000.
3. Sell a kidney for $5,000,000.

Situation 1, donation of human organs, is what is now done in the United States. Is that exploitive? Economists would say "no," as long as the donation is voluntary. Clearly those who argue monetary exchanges for kidneys should not be allowed, but who view donated kidneys as a good thing, must not view donators as exploited. So if a seller is not exploited at a price of zero dollars, how can a seller be exploited at a price of $5,000, or at any price? Or if a seller is not exploited at a really high price like $5,000,000, how can a seller be exploited just because he or she voluntarily accepts a lower price like $5,000 for the kidney?

The second reason for interfering in exchanges between private individuals is what the authors call *meddlesome preferences*. Meddlesome preferences are involved when someone else cares about an exchange that takes place between two other people. An example used in the text is the prohibition in some U.S. states on serving horse meat in restaurants. Horse meat is on the menu in Europe and Japan. And, of course, beef that is regularly eaten in the United States is off the menu in India. Should the majority (who are opposed to restaurants serving horse meat) be able to keep others from eating horse meat? What about other exchanges? Should the majority be able to prevent homosexual interactions, interracial marriage, some religious rites, or other such private transactions that some people, in this case the majority, do not like? One can begin to see the problem with meddlesome preferences. Meddlesome preferences may clash with other values like liberty and freedom.

The third reason discussed for interfering in the marketplace is fair and equal treatment. What is fair or equal may be very costly. In an example in the book, the authors discuss New York City spending a large sum of money to retrofit old city buses to make them wheelchair accessible. As the authors say in this section, economics cannot answer questions about the sacred or the profane. If your religion tells you that pictures of naked people are bad, then it is irrelevant to you that exchanges involving these products are voluntary among other people. You may even think that such exchanges should be banned. If equality in outcomes is your highest value, you may not care what economics says about the costs and benefits of assuring equal outcomes.

The fourth reason the authors give for restricting market choices is cultural goods and paternalism. An example is when a country like Canada discriminates in favor of domestically produced programming on government-owned television. The criticism is that such subsidy schemes tend to be counterproductive and wasteful. Canadian program producers might make better programs, if they had to compete for airtime with shows from the United States.

The fifth reason the authors explore for barring some exchanges is that one may not like the poverty, inequality, or income distribution that results from free exchanges. The authors turn to moral philosophy to help discuss the question of what is a just distribution of wealth.

Rawls's maximin principle says that government, without violating people's basic rights, should maximize the benefit accruing to the most disadvantaged group in society. A person with a **utilitarian** philosophy would argue that we should try to implement outcomes that bring the greatest sum of utility or happiness to society. **Nozick's entitlement theory** posits that the outcome does not matter. What matters is that the process leading to the outcome is just. That is, as long as the trades that lead to one person having more and another person less are truly voluntary, they are moral.

Consider the following table showing the incomes of two different three-person societies.

Table 20.1

Society	Person 1	Person 2	Person 3	Average Income
A	$25,000	$20,000	$15,000	$20,000
B	$40,000	$25,000	$10,000	$25,000

A believer in the Rawls's maximin principle would prefer society A, which has a higher income for the poorest person than society B does. Someone who believed in Nozick's entitlement theory would prefer neither society based on outcomes, because to this person only a fair process matters.

Since utilitarians are looking to maximize total society happiness, they would at times favor redistribution. So they would want some amount of money redistributed from the wealthy to the poor. But taking money from those who created the wealth reduces their incentive to create more wealth, which would make the entire society worse off. Because this outcome acts as a check on the redistributive impulses of utilitarians, we cannot know whether they would prefer society A or B in the previous table.

Next, consider the same two societies with a third three-person society added in, as shown in the following table. A believer in Rawls's maximin principle would prefer

Table 20.2

Society	Person 1	Person 2	Person 3	Average Income
A	$25,000	$20,000	$15,000	$20,000
B	$40,000	$25,000	$10,000	$25,000
C	$1,000,000	$150,000	$50,000	$400,000

society C despite its highly unequal distribution of income. Rawlsians would pick that society because it was the highest income for the poorest person. Again, someone who believed in Nozick's entitlement theory would prefer none of these societies based on outcomes, because to them only a fair process matters. Finally, we cannot know which society utilitarians would pick because of they trade-off they make between happiness maximization and incentives for wealth creation.

The sixth and final reason the authors examine for interfering in private exchanges is who counts. Economists generally would count everyone involved in a decision. Politically though, people who do not live in or vote in a country do not count as much. This factor comes into play when a firm wants to hire someone from another country. The government may prohibit this exchange even though both sides want to make it.

So while economists generally argue that almost any voluntary exchange should be allowed, the majority or the government sometimes prohibits certain exchanges. This chapter identifies and evaluates some of the reasons third parties use to justify interfering with exchanges between two other individuals.

Key Terms

positive economics the economics that explain, explain, or predict without making recommendations

normative economics recommendations or arguments about what economic policy should be

Rawls's maximin principle the principle that says that justice requires maximizing the benefit going to society's most disadvantaged group

Utilitarianism the idea that the best society maximizes the sum of utility

Nozick's entitlement theory of justice a theory that says that the distribution of income in a society is just if property is justly acquired and voluntarily exchanged.

Traps, Hints, and Reminders

Positive economics is about what is. An example of a positive economic statement is: If you raise price, quantity demanded will fall.

Normative economics is about what should be. An example of a normative economic statement is: A person should not be able to sell his or her kidney.

Voluntary exchange makes people or sides better off. Why government might interfere with private exchange are (1) possible exploitation; (2) meddlesome preferences; (3) fairness or equal treatment; (4) protecting cultural goods and paternalism and (5) the poverty, inequality, and unequal distribution of income that can result from free exchanges, leading to the issue of whether some people should count more than others.

Homework Quiz

1. Positive economics is about
   a. what is.
   b. what should be.
   c. what is yet to be discovered in economics.
   d. macroeconomics.

2. Which of the following is a normative economic statement?

a. Drug companies' profits rose last year.

b. Drug companies should lower prices.

c. If demand falls, drug company prices will fall.

d. All of the answers are correct.

Table 20.3

Society	Person 1	Person 2	Person 3	Average Income
A	$75,000	$15,000	$15,000	$35,000
B	$40,000	$30,000	$20,000	$30,000

3. In the preceding table, Society A would be preferred by

a. a Rawlsian.

b. a utilitarian.

c. a believer in Nozick's entitlement theory.

d. None of the answers is correct.

4. In the preceding table, Society B would be preferred by

a. a Rawlsian.

b. a utilitarian.

c. a believer in Nozick's entitlement theory.

d. None of the answers is correct.

5. Nozick's entitlement theory says that

a. justice requires maximizing the benefits going to society's most disadvantaged group.

b. the best society maximizes the sum of utility of all members of that society.

c. the distribution of income in a society is just if property is justly acquired and voluntarily exchanged.

d. the distribution of income is just only if everyone has the same income level.

6. Meddlesome preferences often conflict with

a. the majority.

b. cultural goods.

c. other values like freedom and liberty.

d. All of the answers are correct.

7. Some people do not believe in interfering in the marketplace, because as long as there is no market failure, the market

a. does not maximize total surplus.

b. does not count everyone.

c. produces an efficient amount of the good.

d. All of the answers are correct.

8. A believer in Rawls's principle believes that the government should
   a. maximize the benefit accruing to the most disadvantaged group in society.
   b. maximize total happiness in society.
   c. ensure a just process to societal outcomes.
   d. All of the answers are correct.

9. A believer in a utilitarian society believes that the government should
   a. maximize the benefit accruing to the most disadvantaged group in society.
   b. maximize total happiness in society.
   c. ensure a just process to societal outcomes.
   d. All of the answers are correct.

10. A believer in Nozick's entitlement theory believes the government should
   a. maximize the benefit accruing to the most disadvantaged group in society.
   b. maximize total happiness in society.
   c. ensure a just process to societal outcomes.
   d. All of the answers are correct.

Table 20.4

Society	Person 1	Person 2	Person 3	Average Income
A	$10,000	$10,000	$10,000	$10,000
B	$50,000	$40,000	$30,000	$40,000
C	$70,000	$60,000	$20,000	$50,000

11. Of the three societies in the preceding table, a Rawlsian would prefer
   a. society A.
   b. society B.
   c. society C.
   d. Not enough information is given to be able to make a choice.

12. Of the three societies in the preceding table, a utilitarian would prefer
   a. society A.
   b. society B.
   c. society C.
   d. Not enough information is given to be able to make a choice.

13. Of the three societies in the preceding table, a believer in Nozick's entitlement theory would prefer
   a. society A.
   b. society B.
   c. society C.
   d. Not enough information is given to choose.

14. Utilitarians might favor only a modest redistribution of income

    a. if wealth creators are very sensitive to incentives.

    b. to be fair.

    c. if property is justly acquired.

    d. All of the answers are correct.

15. To an economist, which of the following people would count when evaluating a policy?

    a. an immigrant who wants to enter the United States for a job

    b. the owners of the United States firm who want to hire the immigrant

    c. the competing worker who would also like the job

    d. All of the people described would count.

Self-Practice Questions

1. Normative economics is about

    a. what is.

    b. what should be.

    c. old economic ideas that have been shown to be wrong.

    d. microeconomics.

2. Which of the following is a positive economic statement?

    a. The price of sugar is too high.

    b. People should use less sugar in their diets.

    c. If the price of sugar rises, then the quantity of sugar demanded will fall.

    d. All of the answers are correct.

Table 20.5

Society	Person 1	Person 2	Person 3	Average Income
A	$25,000	$20,000	$15,000	$20,000
B	$40,000	$25,000	$10,000	$25,000

3. In the preceding table, Society A would be preferred by

    a. a Rawlsian.

    b. a utilitarian.

    c. a believer in Nozick's entitlement theory.

    d. None of the answers is correct.

4. In the preceding table, Society B would be preferred by
   a. a Rawlsian.
   b. a utilitarian.
   c. a believer in Nozick's entitlement theory.
   d. None of the answers is correct.

5. Someone who believes that a just process is more important than outcomes is
   a. a Rawlsian.
   b. a utilitarian.
   c. a believer in Nozick's entitlement theory.
   d. None of these answers is correct.

6. Some people believe in interfering with private exchange
   a. to protect cultural goods.
   b. because of worries about exploitation.
   c. because of worries about a lack of fairness.
   d. All of the answers are correct.

7. Some people do not believe in interfering in the marketplace, because as long as there is no market failure, the market
   a. maximizes total surplus.
   b. does not count everyone.
   c. does not produce an efficient amount of the good.
   d. All of the answers are correct.

8. A believer in utilitarian society believes the government should
   a. maximize the benefit accruing to the most disadvantaged group in society.
   b. maximize total happiness in society.
   c. ensure that societal outcomes are just.
   d. All of the answers are correct.

9. A believer in Nozick's entitlement theory believes the government should
   a. maximize the benefit accruing to the most disadvantaged group in society.
   b. maximize total happiness in society.
   c. ensure that societal outcomes are just.
   d. All of the answers are correct.

10. A believer in the Rawls's maximin theory
    a. always prefers the most even distribution of income.
    b. may prefer a lower average income as long as the most disadvantaged group is better off.
    c. always wants to minimize the wealth of the most favored group in society.
    d. may want the most disadvantaged group to have the least benefit.

Table 20.6

Society	Person 1	Person 2	Person 3	Average Income
A	$15,000	$20,000	$25,000	$20,000
B	$50,000	$20,000	$20,000	$30,000
C	$15,000	$15,000	$15,000	$15,000

11. Of the three societies in the previous table, a Rawlsian would prefer
    a. society A.
    b. society B.
    c. society C.
    d. Not enough information is given to be able to make a choice.

12. Of the three societies in the previous table, a utilitarian would prefer
    a. society A.
    b. society B.
    c. society C.
    d. Not enough information is given to be able to make a choice.

13. Of the three societies in the previous table, a believer in Nozick's entitlement theory would prefer
    a. society A.
    b. society B.
    c. society C.
    d. Not enough information is given to choose.

14. Utilitarians would redistribute money from the wealthy to poor people until
    a. everyone has the same income.
    b. total society happiness is maximized.
    c. everyone has the same happiness.
    d. All of the answers are correct.

15. To a U.S. politician, which of the following people would count when evaluating a policy?
    a. an immigrant who wants to enter the United States for a job
    b. the owners of the U.S. firm who want to hire the immigrant
    c. the relatives of the immigrant who hope to receive remittances
    d. All of the answers are correct.

Answers to Self-Practice Questions

1. b, Topic: The Case for Exporting Pollution and Importing Kidneys

2. b, Topic: The Case for Exporting Pollution and Importing Kidneys

3. a, Topic: Poverty, Inequality, and the Distribution of Income

4. b, Topic: Poverty, Inequality, and the Distribution of Income

5. c, Topic: Poverty, Inequality, and the Distribution of Income

6. d, Topic: Meddlesome Preferences

7. a, Topic: Fair and Equal Treatment

8. b, Topic: Poverty, Inequality, and the Distribution of Income

9. c, Topic: Poverty, Inequality, and the Distribution of Income

10. b, Topic: Poverty, Inequality, and the Distribution of Income

11. a, Topic: Poverty, Inequality, and the Distribution of Income

12. b, Topic: Poverty, Inequality, and the Distribution of Income

13. d, Topic: Poverty, Inequality, and the Distribution of Income

14. b, Topic: Poverty, Inequality, and the Distribution of Income

15. b, Topic: Who Counts? Immigration

21

Managing Incentives

Learning Objectives

This chapter covers how people are affected by incentives. The topics covered in this chapter include:

> Lesson One: You Get What You Pay For

> Lesson Two: Tie Pay to Performance to Reduce Risk

> Lesson Three: Money Isn't Everything

Summary

Incentives matter. When an organization gets incentives right, it gets positive outcomes. When an organization gets incentives wrong, it can get very perverse outcomes.

A key concept of incentives is "you get what you pay for." This means that you should be careful to structure incentives toward your direct goal. For example, businesses sometimes pay production workers a **piece rate**. A piece-rate system is any system that pays workers directly for their output. Such an incentive system directly targets output, which is what the firm wants from some production workers. There are, however, issues of quality and team production, which means a piece-rate system is not the best for all production workers.

A piece-rate system encourages existing workers to work harder and to miss less work. It also attracts more productive workers. However, firms must convince workers that more production will not lead to a lower piece rate.

A second key concept of incentives is that under certain circumstances weak incentives work better than strong incentives. Strong incentives put more risk on the worker. When factors the worker does not control affect output, then strong incentives may not translate into more or better effort. Weak incentives may also allow the owner to insure workers against the risk of those factors beyond their control.

An interesting type of weak incentive is a **tournament** in which payment is linked to performance. Thus, a firm can link bonuses to relative rather than total individual sales. Tournaments, however, still reduce the incentive to cooperate. Professors who grade competitively or on a curve have set up a tournament for grades.

A third key concept of incentives is that money is not everything. Incentives are powerful but not all powerful incentives are monetary. Organizations have a **corporate culture** that is the shared collection of values and norms that govern how people interact in the organization or firm. Workers who identify with their organization work harder. Employees who own stock in the firm they work for and members of teams, such as the military (or sport teams), all tend to work harder to support the organization with which they identify.

Key Terms

piece rate any payment system that pays workers directly for their output

tournament a compensation scheme in which payment is based on relative performance

corporate culture the shared collection of values and norms that govern how people interact in an organization or firm

Traps, Hints, and Reminders

You get what you pay for, so it is important to set incentives to pay for what you actually want.

Weak incentives may be better than strong incentives when factors beyond the control of the worker affect output.

Money is not everything. Nonmonetary incentives, such as identification with the company or personal recognition, can be very effective at motivating workers, particularly when combined with monetary incentives.

Some incentives, like tournaments, may discourage cooperation among workers or students in a class.

Homework Quiz

1. It is a truth about incentives that
    a. you get what you pay for.
    b. strong incentives always work best.
    c. money is the only incentive that really works.
    d. All of the answers are correct.

2. It is a truth about incentives that
    a. a company cannot really affect worker behavior.
    b. strong incentives always work best.
    c. nonmonetary incentives can be important.
    d. All of the answers are correct.

3. A piece rate is when a worker is paid
    a. by the number of hours he or she works.
    b. by the amount of output he or she produces.
    c. by the amount the firm produces.
    d. a share of the firm's profit.

4. A tournament encourages effort by
    a. making effort more fun.
    b. encouraging cooperation among workers.
    c. having workers compete for a fixed pool of rewards.
    d. making effort harder to measure.

5. Tournaments have been used to increase effort in
    a. golf.
    b. classrooms.
    c. sales.
    d. All of the answers are correct.

6. Weak incentives can
    a. reduce the risk workers face from factors they cannot control.
    b. discourage worker cooperation.
    c. increase the risk workers face from the external environment.
    d. All of the answers are correct.

7. Weak incentives can
    a. increase the risk workers face from factors they cannot control.
    b. encourage worker cooperation.
    c. increase the risk workers face from the external environment.
    d. All of the answers are correct.

8. Tournaments

   a. encourage players to cooperate.

   b. make outside standards of achievement more important.

   c. have fixed prizes.

   d. All of the answers are correct.

9. Tournaments

   a. encourage players to compete against each other.

   b. make outside standards of achievement irrelevant.

   c. have fixed prizes.

   d. All of the answers are correct.

10. The corporate culture at Walmart led to employees

   a. hiding problems from management.

   b. forming a union.

   c. sharing information with managers who visited the stores regularly.

   d. not getting monetary incentives.

Self-Practice Questions

1. It is a truth about incentives that

   a. a company cannot really affect worker behavior.

   b. weak incentives can encourage worker cooperation.

   c. money is the only incentive that really works.

   d. All of the answers are correct.

2. It is a truth about incentives that

   a. you get what you pay for.

   b. weak incentives can insure workers against things they cannot control.

   c. corporate culture can encourage worker effort.

   d. All of the answers are correct.

3. "You get what you pay for" is a warning that

   a. incentives do not matter.

   b. a firm must be careful in setting up incentives.

   c. incentives must be in terms of money.

   d. All of the answers are correct.

4. In a tournament, the factors that an agent does not control

   a. no longer influence rewards.

   b. have a greater influence on rewards.

c. are controllable by the agent.

d. no longer influence output.

5. With weak incentives

a. workers will face more risk from factors they cannot control.

b. discourage workers from cooperating.

c. the amount of risk workers face from the external environment will be reduced.

d. All of the answers are correct.

6. Weak incentives can

a. reduce the risk workers face from factors they cannot control.

b. encourage worker cooperation.

c. limit the risk workers face from the external environment.

d. All of the answers are correct.

7. Tournaments

a. encourage players to cooperate.

b. make outside standards of achievement irrelevant.

c. give prizes that depend on production.

d. All of the answers are correct.

8. Tournaments

a. encourage players to compete against each other.

b. make outside standards of achievement more important.

c. have prizes that depend on how much is produced.

d. All of the answers are correct.

9. Corporate culture

a. is the statement of company rules in the employee handbook.

b. is the employment laws of a state.

c. is the shared values that govern interaction in an organization.

d. is the natural law of human interaction.

10. An example of a successful corporate culture is

a. most government agencies.

b. the United States military.

c. Kmart.

d. All of the answers are correct.

Answers to Self-Practice Questions

1. b, Topic: Lesson One: You Get What You Pay For

2. d, Topic: Lesson One: You Get What You Pay For

3. b, Topic: Lesson One: You Get What You Pay For

4. a, Topic: Lesson Two: Tie Pay to Performance to Reduce Risk

5. c, Topic: Lesson Two: Tie Pay to Performance to Reduce Risk

6. d, Topic: Lesson Two: Tie Pay to Performance to Reduce Risk

7. b, Topic: Lesson Two: Tie Pay to Performance to Reduce Risk

8. a, Topic: Lesson Two: Tie Pay to Performance to Reduce Risk

9. c, Topic: Lesson Three: Money Isn't Everything

10. b, Topic: Lesson Three: Money Isn't Everything

22

Stock Markets and Personal Finance

Learning Objectives

In this chapter you will learn about stock markets and personal investing. The topics covered include:

> Passive vs. Active Investing

> How to Really Pick Stocks, Seriously

> Other Benefits and Costs of Stock Markets

Summary

A mutual fund buys assets with money pooled from many customers. With **passive investing,** a saver buys a mutual fund that mimics a broad stock market index such as the Standard and Poor's 500 (S&P 500). With **active investing,** a saver buys a mutual fund that is run by managers who try to pick stocks to beat broad market indexes. Active investing has not been shown to give the saver a higher return than passive investing, however.

The **efficient markets hypothesis** says that the prices of traded assets reflect all publicly available information. This implies that it will be difficult for mutual fund managers to actually beat the broad market indexes. Only if you have information not in the market can you beat the market. Additionally, once you start buying or selling, based on that information, the market price will soon reflect your information.

The textbook authors offer four pieces of advice for savers who want to put their savings at risk. The first piece of advice is to diversify: that is, buy a variety of different assets so you do not have all your eggs in one basket.

The second piece of advice is that since the efficient markets hypothesis says that you cannot beat the market by stock picking, your best strategy is to **buy and hold** your diversified assets.

The third piece of advice is to avoid high brokerage fees. In other words, since the efficient markets hypothesis says that you cannot beat the market, do not pay high fees for stock-picking advice.

The fourth and final piece of advice is related to the buy and hold strategy, which is holding your diversified portfolio over a long period to take advantage of the power of compound returns to build wealth. The rule of 70 shows that a small difference in growth rates can lead to a large difference in wealth over decades. This rule states that an annual growth rate divided into 70 tells you the number of years it takes the growing asset to double in value. The textbook thus advises you to not try to beat the market, but to avoid high brokerage fees when buying, and holding, a well-diversified portfolio of assets for a long period advantage of the compounding of returns, which is what builds wealth.

Risk and return are related. The **risk-return trade-off** means higher returns come at the price of higher risk. For example, U.S. government T-bills are safe but have low return; corporate bonds earn a higher return than T-bills but are riskier. By riskier, the textbook means that corporate bond values fluctuate more than T-bill values. The S&P 500 has a higher return than corporate bonds, but the S&P is riskier than corporate bonds. Shares of stock in small companies have returns that are even higher than the S&P 500, but, they are riskier than the S&P 500. Risk implies that the value of an asset can go either up or down and also could, in the extreme, go to zero.

Stock markets are important since companies can use them to raise funds for start-up or expansion. Stock markets use stock prices to signal how well a company is being run. Finally, stock markets are a way of transferring control of a company from less competent people to more competent people.

Bubbles occur when asset prices are bid up higher than the underlying value of the asset. Eventually, however, a bubble must burst and then prices must fall to reflect the true value of the underlying asset. The bursting of price bubbles has sometimes been associated with recession.

Key Terms

efficient markets hypothesis the prices of traded assets reflect all publicly available information

buy and hold buying stocks and then holding them for the long run, regardless of what prices do in the short run

risk-return trade-off higher returns come at the price of higher risk

Traps, Hints, and Reminders

Sometimes students get confused about the trade-off between risk and return. They do not understand why the relationship exists. Imagine that there were two bonds you could buy. One is more risky than the other. Which would you pay more for? The less risky one, of course. But paying more for the less risky bond means that bond has a lower return.

The efficient markets hypothesis is similar to the idea that there is no such thing as a free lunch. If you could easily gather special information on stocks and make money, everyone would do that. That would get rid of your advantage.

Bubbles misallocate resources. For example, if there is a real estate bubble, then resources that would have gone to produce something else are drawn into real estate. This does not mean that investing in housing is bad; it means that consumers valued something else more, and that investors were confused.

The authors do suggest ways to get rich slow. For example, by using the power of compounding, the longer your money is invested, the bigger it will be at the end. Small amounts of money saved over a long period of time can be much bigger than large amounts of money invested for a short period of time. Another way to get rich slow is by diversifying your portfolio to protect yourself against the risk from single stocks. It also helps build your wealth when you can avoid high fees when choosing stocks.

Homework Quiz

1. You are actively investing when you
   a. buy and hold.
   b. try to beat the market.
   c. buy mutual funds that try to mimic broad market indexes.
   d. All of these answers are correct.

2. If you buy and hold a diversified portfolio of assets, you are engaging in
   a. active investment.
   b. passive investment.
   c. foolish investment.
   d. beating the market.

3. The Standard & Poor's 500 is
   a. a NASCAR event.
   b. a narrow index of U.S. bond prices.
   c. a broad index of U.S. stock prices.
   d. an international index of stock prices.

4. The efficient markets hypothesis says that
   a. because big firms are more efficient, they make all the money in stock markets.
   b. the prices of trade assets reflect all publicly available information.
   c. big firms are more efficient at picking stocks than individual investors.
   d. individuals are better at picking stocks than big firms.

5. Your stockbroker tells you that today's news means that Google will make much more money next year than anyone had predicted. He recommends a buy. Why might this be poor advice?

   a. He is just trying to unload his own stock.

   b. If it was in today's news, the price has already increased.

   c. Newspapers usually try to manipulate the stock market for their own gain.

   d. None of the answers is correct.

6. After the nuclear power plant in Chernobyl melted down and contaminated the Ukraine with radiation, American potato prices increased because

   a. people wanted to eat more potatoes.

   b. people were afraid to buy stocks.

   c. people were afraid to buy bonds.

   d. traders quickly realized that since Ukrainian potatoes were contaminated, American potato prices would rise.

7. The authors' advice for picking stock includes

   a. focus on one asset.

   b. buy and hold assets for long periods of time.

   c. pay what it takes to get advice from the best stock pickers.

   d. frequently dump some assets and buy others.

8. The authors' advice for picking stock includes

   a. diversify or hold many different assets.

   b. change the assets in your portfolio frequently.

   c. pay what it takes to get advice from the best stock pickers.

   d. only hold your portfolio for a short period of time.

9. The authors' advice for picking stock includes

   a. diversify or hold many different assets.

   b. avoid paying high brokerage fees.

   c. take advantage of compounding returns to build wealth.

   d. All of the answers are correct.

10. The rule of 70 implies that if an asset's annual growth rate is 2 percent, then the asset will double in value in

    a. 2 years.

    b. 35 years.

    c. 140 years.

    d. It will never double in value.

11. According to diversification, if you work in the auto industry you should
    a. invest heavily in auto stocks.
    b. split your portfolio equally between auto stocks and nonauto stocks.
    c. have relatively few auto stocks.
    d. buy companies that supply auto companies.

12. Rank the following asset categories from lowest risk to highest risk.
    a. U.S. T-bills, small stocks, S&P 500, corporate bonds
    b. corporate bonds, small stocks, S&P 500, T-bills
    c. U.S. T-bills, corporate bonds, S&P 500, small stocks
    d. U.S. T-bills, small stocks, corporate bonds, S&P 500

13. The relationship between risk and return of an asset is
    a. that as returns rise, so does risk.
    b. an inverse relationship.
    c. a negative relationship.
    d. that as return rise, risk falls.

14. When economists talk about bubbles they mean that
    a. you never know what will happen to the economy.
    b. sometimes markets bid up prices well above the value of the underlying asset.
    c. sometimes market participants spend too much time focusing on core competencies.
    d. sometimes stock prices float back and forth like soap bubbles.

15. Bubble bursts are hard on economies because
    a. the bubble led people to put resources in the wrong areas.
    b. people do not like to let asset prices get too high or too low.
    c. bubbles are not actually painful, since paper profits may go up and then down, but only on paper.
    d. the bubbles caused people to not buy assets before they burst.

Self-Practice Questions

1. Passive investing is when you
   a. buy and hold stocks.
   b. try to beat the market.
   c. buy mutual funds run by stock pickers who have a solid record of beating the market.
   d. All of the answers are correct.

2. If you pick stocks to try to beat the market, you are engaging in

a. active investment.

b. passive investment.

c. conservative investment.

d. illegal investment.

3. The idea that the prices of traded assets reflect all publicly available information is known as

a. a speculative bubble.

b. beating the market.

c. diversification.

d. the efficient markets hypothesis.

4. Your friend calls you with news from the morning paper that should make a certain stock more valuable. You should

a. buy the stock and reap the reward.

b. sell the stock because the paper is wrong.

c. not buy or sell the stock because the information would already be reflected in the price of the stock soon after the paper was printed.

d. not buy or sell the stock because this would be insider trading.

5. When financial economists talk about a stock's risk, they mean

a. how much the stock's price moves up and down.

b. how much the stock's price moves up or down compared to its previous movement.

c. how the stock's price moves up or down along with the rest of the market.

d. how high the price of the stock is.

6. The fall of a stock market price means that

a. the stock is undervalued and its price will rise.

b. the stock's price will continue to fall.

c. most buyers and sellers negatively reevaluated their opinion of the stock.

d. the stock's price will suddenly have more variance.

7. The text authors' advice for picking assets is to

a. trade frequently.

b. buy and hold assets for only short periods of time.

c. avoid paying high brokerage fees.

d. buy only one type of asset.

8. One piece of advice for picking assets that the text authors give is to

a. buy and hold a well-diversified portfolio of assets.

b. avoid paying high brokerage fees.

c. take advantage of compounding returns to build wealth.

d. All of the answers are correct.

9. Diversification means that if, for example, you work in the banking industry, you should
   a. invest heavily in bank stocks.
   b. split your portfolio equally between bank stocks and nonbank stocks.
   c. have relatively few bank stocks.
   d. buy stock only in financial companies.

10. Corporate bond returns are higher than the returns on
    a. T-bills.
    b. the S&P 500.
    c. shares of stock in small companies.
    d. All of the answers are correct.

11. If the return on corporate bonds rises, then you would expect the risk of corporate bonds to
    a. fall.
    b. rise.
    c. be unaffected.
    d. be unpredictable.

12. A bubble in a market is when the market price
    a. rises rapidly.
    b. falls rapidly.
    c. rises above the value of the underlying asset.
    d. is undervalued.

13. The rule of 70 implies that if an asset's annual growth rate is 5%, then the asset will double its value in
    a. 14 years.
    b. 70 years.
    c. 350 years.
    d. no specified amount of time.

14. If S&P 500 risk falls, then you would expect the return from the S&P 500 to
    a. fall.
    b. rise.
    c. be unaffected.
    d. be unpredictable.

15. Stock markets
    a. are where companies raise funds for start up or expansion.
    b. signal when companies are poorly managed.
    c. facilitate transfer of company control from less competent to more competent people.
    d. All of the answers are correct.

Answers to Self-Practice Questions

1. a, Topic: Passive vs. Active Investing

2. a, Topic: Passive vs. Active Investing

3. d, Topic: Passive vs. Active Investing

4. c, Topic: Passive vs. Active Investing

5. a, Topic: Passive vs. Active Investing

6. c, Topic: Passive vs. Active Investing

7. c, Topic: How to Really Pick Stocks, Seriously

8. d, Topic: How to Really Pick Stocks, Seriously

9. c, Topic: How to Really Pick Stocks, Seriously

10. a, Topic: How to Really Pick Stocks, Seriously

11. b, Topic: How to Really Pick Stocks, Seriously

12. c, Topic: How to Really Pick Stocks, Seriously

13. a, Topic: How to Really Pick Stocks, Seriously

14. a, Topic: How to Really Pick Stocks, Seriously

15. d, Topic: Other Benefits and Costs of Stock Markets

23

Consumer Choice

Learning Objectives

In this chapter, which covers consumer choice, you will look underneath the demand curve and see from where demand comes. The topics covered include:

> How to Compare Apples and Oranges
> The Demand Curve
> The Budget Constraint
> Preferences and Indifference Curves
> Optimization and Consumer Choice
> The Income and Substitution Effect
> Applications of Income and Substitution Effect

Summary

What the consumer gets from a good is utility. As in the rest of this book, we are here interested in marginal analysis. **Marginal utility** is the change in total utility that occurs from consuming an additional unit. We expect that each additional unit of a good consumed adds less to the utility than the previous unit consumed, or that there is **diminishing marginal utility.**

The **optimal consumption rule** states that to maximize utility, a consumer should allocate spending so the marginal utility per dollar is equal for all purchases. Thus, if the $[MU_{candy}/P_{candy}] > [MU_{pizza}/P_{pizza}]$ for a consumer, the consumer can increase his or her total utility by buying less pizza and more candy. The reason is that the utility he or she gives up, MU_{pizza}/P_{pizza}, is smaller than the utility they gain, MU_{candy}/P_{candy}.

From the optimal consumption rule, we can see the demand relationship. If the $[MU_{candy}/P_{candy}] = [MU_{pizza}/P_{pizza}]$ and the price of candy rises, then $[MU_{candy}/P_{candy}] < [MU_{pizza}/P_{pizza}]$ and the consumer will react to the increase in the price of candy by purchasing less candy.

A **budget constraint** shows all the consumption bundles that a consumer can afford, given the consumer's income and the price of goods. Because the slope of the budget constraint shows the relative prices of the goods, the budget constraint tells us what the consumer can actually do in the marketplace. In Figure 23.1, the budget constraint starts with budget constraint *AB*. If the price of pizza rises, then the budget constraint would pivot to a budget constraint such as *AC*. If income falls, the budget constraint will shift from budget constraint *AB* to a budget constraint such as *EC*.

Figure 23.1

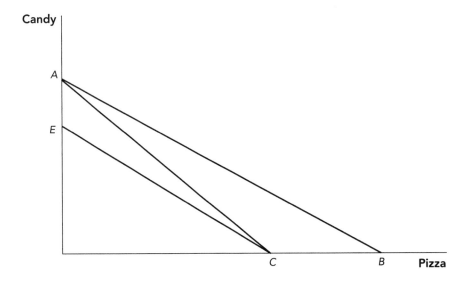

Remembering that the budget constraint shows what the consumer can do in the marketplace, we need to determine what the consumer wants to do. We do this by using indifference curves. Indifference curves are different combinations of goods that provide the consumer with the same total utility. The slope of these curves is the marginal rate of substitution. The **marginal rate of substitution (MRS)** is the rate at which the consumer is willing to trade one good for another and remain indifferent. The *MRS* is the slope of the indifference curve.

Optimal choice is the situation in which the consumer maximizes utility, subject to the consumer's budget constraint. The *MRS*, i.e., the slope of the indifference curve, is equal to the slope of the budget constraint at the optimum choice. At point *A* in Figure 23.2, the indifference curve is steeper than the budget constraint, so that $[MU_{pizza}/MU_{candy}] > [P_{pizza}/P_{candy}]$. By cross-multiplying, we see that $[MU_{pizza}/P_{pizza}] > [MU_{candy}/P_{candy}]$; thus, to maximize utility, the consumer should buy more pizza and less candy. At point *C* in Figure 23.2, the indifference curve is flatter than the budget constraint, so $[MU_{pizza}/MU_{candy}] < [P_{pizza}/P_{candy}]$. By cross-multiplying, we see that $[MU_{pizza}/P_{pizza}] < [MU_{candy}/P_{candy}]$ and so, to maximize utility, the consumer should buy more candy and less pizza. At point *B* in Figure 23.2, the slope of the indifference

Figure 23.2

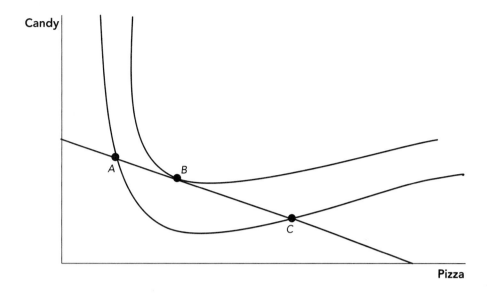

curve is equal to the slope of the budget constraint, so $[MU_{pizza}/MU_{candy}] = [P_{pizza}/P_{candy}]$. By cross-multiplying, we see that $[MU_{pizza}/P_{pizza}] = [MU_{candy}/P_{candy}]$, and, as the optimal consumption rule predicts, the consumer is maximizing utility subject to the budget constraint.

A change in a price affects a consumer's real income. Because of this change in real income, the total effect of a price change can be broken up into substitution and income effects. The **substitution effect** is the change in consumption caused by a change in relative prices, holding the consumer's utility level constant. The **income effect** is the change in consumption caused by a change in purchasing power from a price change. In figure 23.3, if the consumer starts with budget constraint AB, he or she consumes S_1 shirts. If the price of shirts falls, as shown in budget constraint AF, the consumer consumption of shirts rises to S_3. The change from S_1 to S_3 is the total effect. Because the

Figure 23.3

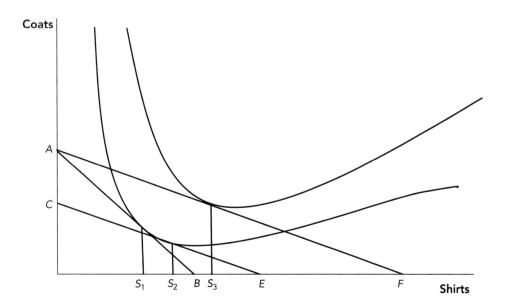

graph shows budget constraint *CE*, reflecting the new prices, the original level of utility, the total effect, can be broken down into the substitution and income effects. The substitution effect is the movement along the indifference curve or the change in shirt consumption from S_1 to S_2. The income effect is the movement due to the parallel shift of the budget constraint, or the change in shirt consumption from S_2 to S_3.

The ideas of income and substitution effects can be used in many economic situations. If you lose a ticket to a movie, the relative price of movies has not changed and your income probably has not changed much, so you may as well just buy another ticket to replace the lost one. But, if you lose a more expensive ticket, for example, a $100 Muse ticket, depending on your income level your income may change enough that your income effect causes you not to replace the Muse ticket. Income and substitution effects can be analyzed by the optimal membership fee at membership stores like Sam's Club.

The tools in this chapter can also be used to describe the labor–leisure trade-off. If your wages rise, then you have both an income and a substitution effect. The substitution effect of a wage increase will make you want to work more. The income effect of a wage increase will make you want to work less and enjoy more leisure. If the substitution effect of a wage increase is greater than the negative income effect, then the person's labor supply curve will be upward sloping. However, if the substitution effect of a wage increase is less than the negative income effect, then the person's labor supply curve will be negatively sloped. Similarly, welfare programs need to be carefully constructed because those that merely increase income will induce recipients of the payments to work less or not at all.

Key Terms

marginal utility the change in utility from consuming an additional unit

diminishing marginal utility each additional unit of a good consumed adds less to utility than the previous unit

optimal consumption rule to maximize utility, a consumer should allocate spending, so the marginal utility per dollar is equal for all purchases

budget constraint all of the consumption bundles that a consumer can afford, given income and the prices

marginal rate of substitution (MRS) the rate at which the consumer is willing to trade one good for another and remain indifferent

substitution effect the change in consumption caused by a change in relative prices, holding the consumer's utility level constant

income effect the change in consumption caused by a change in purchasing power from a price change

Traps, Hints, and Reminders

The budget constraint shows what the consumer can do in the marketplace.

Indifference curves show what the consumer wants to do in his or her consumption.

The consumer optimum is determined by the tension between what the consumer wants to do and what the consumer can do.

Homework Quiz

1. A change in utility from consuming one more unit is
   a. the optimal consumption rule.
   b. the income effect.
   c. the consumer optimum.
   d. marginal utility.

2. The optimal consumption rule says
   a. to maximize utility, a consumer should allocate spending, so the marginal utility per dollar is equal for all purchases.
   b. the consumer is willing to trade one good for another and remain indifferent.
   c. there is a change in utility from consuming one more unit.
   d. All of the answers are correct.

3. If $[MU_{soda}/P_{soda}] > [MU_{pizza}/P_{pizza}]$, a consumer can increase his or her total utility by
   a. buying more pizza and less soda.
   b. buying more soda and less pizza.
   c. buying more of both goods.
   d. The consumer is at his or her optimum and cannot increase total utility.

Figure 23.4

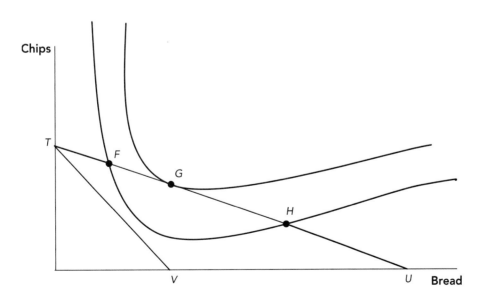

4. In Figure 23.4, the consumer optimum is point
   a. *F.*   c. *H.*
   b. *G.*   d. None of the answers is correct.

5. In Figure 23.4, the movement from budget constraint TU to budget constraint TV can be caused by a(n)

   a. decrease in income.

   b. increase in the price of chips.

   c. increase in the price of bread.

   d. decrease in the price of bread.

6. In Figure 23.4, at point F

   a. $[MU_{bread}/P_{bread}] > [MU_{chips}/P_{chips}]$.

   b. $[MU_{bread}/P_{bread}] = [MU_{chips}/P_{chips}]$.

   c. $[MU_{bread}/P_{bread}] < [MU_{chips}/P_{chips}]$.

   d. the relationship between $[MU_{bread}/P_{bread}]$ and $[MU_{chips}/P_{chips}]$ is unknown.

7. In Figure 23.4, at the consumer optimum

   a. $MU_{bread} = MU_{chips}$.

   b. $P_{bread} = P_{chips}$.

   c. $[MU_{bread}/P_{bread}] = [MU_{chips}/P_{chips}]$.

   d. All of the answers are correct.

Figure 23.5

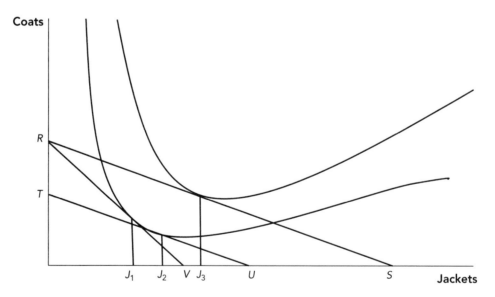

8. In Figure 23.5, if the consumer starts with budget constraint RV, the total effect of the price change is the movement of

   a. J_1 to J_2.

   b. J_1 to J_3.

   c. J_2 to J_3.

   d. None of the answers is correct.

9. In Figure 23.5, if the consumer starts with budget constraint *RV*, the substitution effect of the price change is the movement of

   a. J_1 to J_2.

   b. J_1 to J_3.

   c. J_2 to J_3.

   d. None of the answers is correct.

10. In Figure 23.5, if the consumer starts with budget constraint *RV,* the income effect of the price change is the movement of

   a. J_1 to J_2.

   b. J_1 to J_3.

   c. J_2 to J_3.

   d. None of the answers is correct.

11. A substitution effect is

   a. the rate at which the consumer is willing to trade one good for another and remain indifferent.

   b. the change in consumption caused by a change in relative prices, holding the consumer's utility level constant.

   c. the change in consumption caused by a change in purchasing power from a price change.

   d. None of the answers is correct.

12. The change in consumption caused by a change in purchasing power from a price change is the

   a. marginal rate of substitution.

   b. substitution effect.

   c. income effect.

   d. total effect.

13. If you lose your ticket to a movie, then you will

   a. always replace the ticket.

   b. replace the ticket unless it is so costly that it causes a large income effect.

   c. never replace the ticket.

   d. replace the ticket when the ticket is cheap enough that it causes a large substitution effect.

14. The labor supply curve is negatively sloped if the income effect of a wage

   a. increase is equal to the substitution effect.

   b. change is smaller than the substitution effect.

   c. change is larger than the substitution effect.

   d. change is positive.

15. Welfare programs that pay people

    a. increase recipient hours of work due to an income effect.

    b. decrease recipient hours of work due to an income effect.

    c. increase recipient hours of work due to a substitution effect.

    d. decrease recipient hours of work due to a substitution effect.

Self-Practice Questions

1. Marginal utility is

    a. when, in order to maximize utility, a consumer allocates spending, so the marginal utility per dollar is equal for all purchases.

    b. the rate at which the consumer is willing to trade one good for another and remain indifferent.

    c. a change in utility from consuming one more unit.

    d. All of the answers are correct.

2. In order to maximize utility, a consumer should allocate spending, so the marginal utility per dollar is equal for all purchases. This is called

    a. the optimal consumption rule.

    b. the income effect.

    c. the consumer optimum.

    d. marginal utility.

3. If $[MU_{soda}/P_{soda}] < [MU_{chips}/P_{chips}]$, a consumer can increase his or her total utility by

    a. buying less chips and more soda.

    b. buying more chips and less soda.

    c. buying more of both goods.

    d. The consumer is at his or her optimum and cannot increase total utility.

Figure 23.6

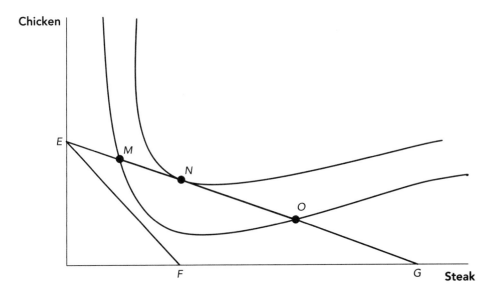

4. In Figure 23.6, the consumer optimum is point

    a. *M.*   c. *O.*

    b. *N.*   d. None of the answers is correct.

5. In Figure 23.6, the movement from budget constraint *EF* to budget constraint *EG* can be caused by a(n)

    a. increase in income.

    b. decrease in the price of chicken.

    c. increase in the price of steak.

    d. decrease in the price of steak.

6. In Figure 23.6, at point *O*

    a. $[MU_{chicken}/P_{chicken}] > [MU_{steak}/P_{steak}]$.

    b. $[MU_{chicken}/P_{chicken}] < [MU_{steak}/P_{steak}]$.

    c. $[MU_{chicken}/P_{chicken}] = [MU_{steak}/P_{steak}]$.

    d. the relationship between $[MU_{chicken}/P_{chicken}]$ and $[MU_{steak}/P_{steak}]$ is unknown.

7. In Figure 23.6, at the consumer optimum

    a. $MU_{chicken} = MU_{steak}$.

    b. $P_{chicken} = P_{steak}$.

    c. $[MU_{chicken}/P_{chicken}] = [MU_{steak}/P_{steak}]$.

    d. All of the answers are correct.

Figure 23.7

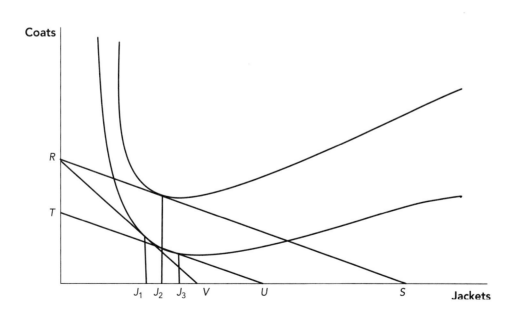

8. In Figure 23.7, if the consumer starts with budget constraint *RV*, the total effect of the price change is the movement of

    a. J_1 to J_2.   c. J_2 to J_3.

    b. J_1 to J_3.   d. None of the answers is correct.

9. In Figure 23.7, if the consumer starts with budget constraint *RV*, the substitution effect of the price change is the movement of

    a. J_1 to J_2.

    b. J_1 to J_3.

    c. J_2 to J_3.

    d. None of the answers is correct.

10. In Figure 23.7, if the consumer starts with budget constraint *RV*, the income effect of the price change is the movement of

    a. J_1 to J_2.

    b. J_1 to J_3.

    c. J_2 to J_3.

    d. None of the answers is correct.

11. An income effect is

    a. the rate at which the consumer is willing to trade one good for another and remain indifferent.

    b. the change in consumption caused by a change in relative prices, holding the consumer's utility level constant.

    c. the change in consumption caused by a change in purchasing power from a price change.

    d. None of the answers is correct.

12. The change in consumption caused by a change in purchasing power from a price change is the

    a. marginal rate of substitution.

    b. substitution effect.

    c. income effect.

    d. total effect.

13. If you lose your ticket to a movie, you will

    a. always replace that ticket.

    b. not replace the ticket when the ticket is cheap enough that it causes a large substitution effect.

    c. never replace the ticket.

    d. not replace the ticket when it is expensive enough to cause a large income effect.

14. The labor supply curve is positively sloped if the income effect of a wage

    a. increase is equal to the substitution effect.

    b. change is smaller than the substitution effect.

    c. change is larger than the substitution effect.

    d. change is positive.

15. The marginal rate of substitution is

    a. the rate at which the consumer is willing to trade one good for another and remain indifferent.

    b. the slope of the indifference curve.

    c. the ratio of the marginal utilities of the two goods.

    d. All of the answers are correct.

Answers to Self-Practice Questions

1. c, Topic: How to Compare Apples and Oranges

2. a, Topic: How to Compare Apples and Oranges

3. b, Topic: The Demand Curve

4. b, Topic: Preference and Consumer Choice

5. d, Topic: The Budget Constraint

6. a, Topic: Preference and Consumer Choice

7. c, Topic: Preference and Consumer Choice

8. a, Topic: The Income and Substitution Effects

9. b, Topic: The Income and Substitution Effects

10. c, Topic: The Income and Substitution Effects

11. c, Topic: The Income and Substitution Effects

12. b, Topic: The Income and Substitution Effects

13. d, Topic: Applications of Income and Substitution Effects

14. b, Topic: Applications of Income and Substitution Effects

15. d, Topic: Preferences and Indifference Curves